"Just reading these stories will give you a confidence boost! Here are thirty-one incredible women with plenty of secrets to share; they'll show you that your journey may have bumps, and it probably won't be a straight path, but if you keep going you will make amazing things happen." —CLAIRE SHIPMAN, coauthor of the *New York Times* bestseller *The Confidence Code for Girls*

"*Girls Who Run the World* is a modern-day encyclopedia of the women who are changing the world today, period." —SOPHIA AMORUSO, cofounder and CEO of Girlboss, a media company dedicated to empowering women in business, and author of the *New York Times* bestseller *#GIRLBOSS*

"*Girls Who Run the World* is a woman-to-woman playbook that spotlights bold businesswomen who have achieved success and done it in their own way. In these pages, Kapp reminds all women that if we work hard as one team and support one another, there is no limit to how far we will go." — MADELEINE K. ALBRIGHT, former secretary of state

"Diana Kapp brings us one of the most important gifts of all: inspiration for the next generation to create lives fueled with equal parts purpose and ambition. This book is a joyful testament to the power of girls, the power of immigrants, and the unlimited potential for young people everywhere to dream boldly." —LAURENE POWELL JOBS, founder of Emerson Collective and cofounder of College Track

"All girls should dare to dream big, and *Girls Who Run the World* gives them the tools not only to achieve those dreams, but to change the world while they're doing it." —ARIANNA HUFFINGTON, founder and CEO of Thrive Global

"The start-up community needs more female and underrepresented founders. Diana Kapp's book is sure to inspire future female founders from all backgrounds to start companies that will change the world. These profiles will give them the tactics and conviction to take a risk on their idea and create a product people will tell their friends about." —SAM ALTMAN, chairperson of Y Combinator and cochairperson of OpenAI

"The book allows us to imagine success by seeing the girl CEOs accomplish it." —GITANJALI RAO, age 14, winner of the Discovery Education 3M Young Scientist Challenge for her device detecting lead in water following the Flint, MI, crisis

GIRLS WHO RUN THE WORLD

31 CEOS WHO
MEAN BUSINESS

BY DIANA KAPP

ILLUSTRATED BY BIJOU KARMAN

Delacorte Press

Library of Congress Cataloging-in-Publication Data is available upon request.
ISBN 978-1-9848-9305-5 (hc) — ISBN 978-0-593-11907-5 (lib. bdg.)
ISBN 978-1-9848-9306-2 (ebook)

The text of this book is set in 10-point Gotham Light.
Interior design by Jaclyn Whalen

MANUFACTURED IN CHINA
10 9 8 7 6 5 4 3 2 1
First Edition

*For my Emma, who was born to run the world,
my intrepid Elliot, and my mom,
the strongest girls I know*

CONTENTS

INTRODUCTION

Although often neglected in history books, girls have been running things behind the scenes forever. The first solar-heated home? Developed by a woman. The daily-appreciated dishwasher? Woman. The creator of the Brooklyn Bridge? Woman again. That clever mistake-cover-upper, Liquid Paper? A woman concocted it in her kitchen blender. The list goes on: windshield wipers, the board game Monopoly, the ice cream maker, even the trusty basic brown bag. All invented by women.

But forget history—there are women out there today who most people have never heard of, breaking barriers this very second.

Back at the beginning of my career, I attended Stanford Graduate School of Business, where I went to learn about turning big ideas into companies to better our world. Sitting in those lecture halls studying the business greats, I kept wondering: Where are the women? Almost all the companies we were being taught to admire were founded by men.

When I graduated, I became a journalist in San Francisco, the beating heart of the tech revolution, covering the truly transformative ideas all around me—stem cells, virtual reality, 3-D printing, driverless cars. Again, I found myself asking: Where are the women? Sure, there are female-founded companies with name recognition, but the few out there succeeding are not visible enough. Not even close.

You may have heard the troubling stats before. There are still so few women at the top. (And it's getting worse—in 2018 the number of female CEOs at top companies *fell* 25 percent from 2017!) Women in business start out equal to men in terms of jobs and pay, but the drop-off begins with the first promotion to management. And businesses founded exclusively by women snag only 2.7 percent of venture capital dollars.

These statistics are begging to be altered. And now is the moment—your moment—to defy them. Venture capitalists (VCs) are desperate to fund females—they need the missing half of our nation's brain cells—but in order for a woman to start the next Apple or Amazon, she needs to believe it is possible. To see herself in that role.

And when girls do land businesses, guess what? Substantial research finds that they *outperform* the guys, which is why venture capitalists are frantic to bring women entrepreneurs into their investment portfolios. A 2013 study of privately held technology companies found those with at least one woman founder have a 35 percent higher return on investment. A 2018 Boston Consulting Group study found that companies led or co-led by women generate 10 percent more in cumulative revenue over a five-year period than those led by all-male teams. They use investment money more efficiently, too: for every dollar of funding, these start-ups generated 78 cents, while male-founded start-ups generated just 31 cents. Why *wouldn't* you bet on female CEOs?

Girls Who Run the World features thirty-one women who defied the statistics and founded awesome businesses, becoming emblems of what is possible. They mastered the art of speaking up and *loud,* they took big risks with big money, they overreached and made mistakes, and ultimately they believed in their own brains, persisted, and hit it big.

In the pages that follow, you'll find real trade secrets from the front lines of CEO life and insider stories that reveal what it's really like to be a woman in business, with millions of dollars at stake.

It's rare to gain this level of access to entrepreneurs, to see how the money and deals get made. I was lucky enough to interview twenty-eight of these thirty-one darn busy ladies, so all this comes straight from them. You will find no candy coating here, no glossing over of trip-ups. The I-wish-I-could-do-that-over moments are on full display. You will learn that there is no straight line to "making bank." Every successful business takes a zigzag course to the top, and every start-up journey is rough, a twenty-four-hour-a-day sprint on a tightrope. Over a fire. In a lightning storm. Just maintaining confidence, let alone a balance in the bank, is a battle. The idea known as Murphy's Law applies: whatever can go wrong, will go wrong. Competitors come out of nowhere. Delivery trucks break down. Checks bounce and employees flake. And yet, as you'll see, all that chaos is what makes being CEO so darn satisfying. You're in the hot seat, solving problems every hour of that daily sprint so that you can say, "I made something, and it matters. I matter."

This book is a strong "yes, please" to moneymaking, an idea that has been pretty taboo for girls for, oh, forever. But until we matter *financially,* our voices won't be heard. And until we understand money—know how much we have, how much we need, how to invest it, account for it, pay taxes on it, and feel comfortable dealing with it—we are going to finish second, behind the boys. Money is tied to power. Money is tied to *everything.* It just is.

So cozy up with these thirty-one hotshots, and you'll start absorbing their can-do spirit. Their wisdom and ways will supercharge you far beyond business, too. Need a confidence boost as you power through your history report? Having trouble believing you can put together a successful election campaign for student council? Revisit the against-all-odds stories gathered here; they will inspire you to go for it, double down, recommit. After all, the tools you need to invent world-changing things are the tools you need for life: doggedness, heart, community, faith, and a candy stash for emergencies.

Girls, you are inventive and powerful. You are the sharpest tacks around. No doubt the next Apple or Amazon will come from someone who looks just like you (it might even *be* you). A girl is going to invent a machine that sucks all the plastic out of the oceans. Another one will mastermind a tiny pill with every critical nutrient, eliminating world hunger. One more will pioneer _____ (fill in the blank).

So here you go, clever girl, natural-born leader. Don't wait. Go run the world.

FASHION/
APPAREL

JENN HYMAN

COFOUNDER AND CEO OF
RENT THE RUNWAY

Business 101: Tap into the zeitgeist. Ownership is out, and the sharing/renting economy is in.

HER BUSINESS: A massive clothes closet for rent, from special-occasion outfits to maternity dresses to work wear to jeans. Pick your duds, pay your money, and the latest fashions arrive on your doorstep.

AN EARLY INSPIRATION: Sara Blakely of Spanx (page 11).

THE THEATRICAL TYPE: As a kid, she wanted to be a singer in a Motown band, a Knicks City Dancer, or a Broadway star. Jenn considers her biggest talent to be remembering lyrics to any song she's heard more than once, and spends (almost) all her waking hours listening to Spotify playlists and singing!

SOME FIGHTING WORDS: "Nothing ever happens by accident or luck—we all have to make it happen by our own energy and assertiveness!"

BOARD MEMBER: In addition to leading the Rent the Runway board, she helps guide the makeup giant Estée Lauder after having been appointed to their board in 2018.

GUINNESS BOOK OF WORLD RECORDS–WORTHY: It is rumored that Rent the Runway has the world's largest dry cleaner! (The smudge of shrimp cocktail sauce or hot fudge drip on that dress has to disappear before the next gal wears it, right?)

FIRST BUSINESS: Selling homemade friendship bracelets on the beach in Hawaii. She put her cutie-pie little sis in front as salesgirl. When making all those bracelets became a pain, they ordered a pile online from Oriental Trading and sold those.

"Buy less stuff" is Jenn's mantra. For a CEO with zillions of designer garments in her New Jersey warehouse, this isn't exactly the retail philosophy you'd expect. But her business is shaking up the old way of buying clothes. Her idea is for women to stop dropping $495 on that cool Reformation trumpet-sleeve cocktail number or lots more for that classy Versace gown, to definitely quit stockpiling fast fashion at Topshop and Zara—and rent instead. "Stop shopping at cheap stores that are producing things with cheap labor that are just going to sit in the back of your closet," she said at a *Recode* (techie news) event.

The concept hit Jenn in 2008 while she was visiting her younger sis, Becky, who had just plunked down more than a month's rent on a cocktail dress, badly boosting her credit-card **debt.** Her sister insisted that it's the social media age, where photos are zapped everywhere, so you *always* need a new outfit. That was the light-bulb moment. Why *own* that dress you'll wear once? She went back to

Harvard Business School and told her friend Jenny Fleiss her idea. Jenny's response: "This sounds fun!"

Their next move was to reach out to the famous dress designer Diane von Furstenberg, to see if she'd partner with them in some way. They didn't know her, so to contact her they just started typing every possible permutation of her name, hoping to guess her email address. Diane@dvf.com . . . ? No. DianeVF@dianevonfurstenberg.com . . . ? No. vonfurstenberg@mac.com . . . ? No.

Tip: A great trick when you don't know someone's email— try guessing. Oftentimes the format is whatever is most obvious. Or call the company and ask for their email address format and plug in the name.

After *many* error messages, one email went through, and shockingly, Diane pinged right back. She invited the pair to her New York office. Driving from Boston in a rental car, they made up their company name. They donned DVF dresses, reached out a hand, and introduced themselves as the cofounders of Rent the Runway.

A second meeting was scheduled. But driving there, forty blocks from the office, Diane's assistant called to say Diane was canceling. Jenn said, "Well, we're just around the corner. We'll pop in briefly." The assistant firmly repeated that Diane didn't want to see them. At that moment, Jenn slyly pretended she didn't

Tip: Don't leave the first meeting without scheduling the second meeting. No "I'll be in touch about dates shortly." Have your calendars out and nail down a date.

hear her. "What? What? You're cutting out," she said. "We'll be there in five minutes." And in they went. Now, that's gutsy! And skillful! Jenn thought, *What's the worst that can happen? If we get escorted out, we'll have a hysterical story!* But the best thing happened: It worked.

At the second meeting, Diane decided she wasn't going to sign on right then as a partner, but if they could sign up lots of other designers, she might participate. Then she gave them a few contacts who might help. To launch, Jenn and Jenny used most of their savings and bought a hundred dresses at Bloomingdale's. They bought in their own sizes, so if all else failed, at least they'd have a killer wardrobe. They set up a pop-up store on the Harvard campus as a test. It was a runaway hit! Because they needed tons of **inventory** to open online, they initially raised $1.75 million from investors. (They have raised much more to date.) They were clever about marketing Rent the Runway from the start. The *Sex and the City* film had opened that summer, and they walked the movie lines at every theater around town, collecting emails.

> **Tip:** When leaving a meeting, ask for two names of people who might be helpful and their contact info. This can turn into a big web of helpfulness.

Rent the Runway is no longer just for party outfits. The company has over 11 million members, and most of the company's subscribers are working women. Jenn's thought: What they need is career clothes! In 2016, Jenn started a monthly subscription service offering a regular supply of work duds and everyday clothing in addition to outfits for special occasions. She keeps adding clothing categories, like maternity wear, bridesmaid dresses, resort wear, even jeans! Rent the Runway's operation is so efficient that they can process one woman's return and have it shipping to someone else in twelve hours. Of the 1,800 employees, hundreds work in logistics! Ninety-eight percent of renters try brands they've never worn. Maybe they'll fall for Tibi, Vince, Lilly Pulitzer, Rag & Bone, or one of the six hundred plus brands stocked.

Her sister insisted that it's the social media age, where photos are zapped everywhere, so you always need a new outfit.

Being a cheerleader for women is a major priority for Jenn. Her passion stems from formative early experiences. At her first job out of college, working for a hotel and travel company, her boss told her to act "sweet" and not to speak much in meetings. Jenn's boldness was "coming across the wrong way." Her initial reaction was to dissolve into tears. But then she heeded a senior colleague who told her, "Keep doing what you're doing. Your boss is going to be working for you one day!" Just after she launched Rent the Runway and appeared on the front page of the *New York Times* business section, Jenn's boyfriend broke up with her, saying he didn't want to be with a powerful career gal. There have been ups and downs learning to be a CEO, but Jenn feels that these are unavoidable growing pains in a rapidly expanding company, and her goal is to keep learning. Her trick is to just keep believing in herself and being who she is, as her coworker advised her so long ago. "Had I decided to listen to [my boss] at that point, we wouldn't be where we are today," she told a *HuffPost* reporter.

Rent the Runway is heavily female and diverse—93 percent of employees are female and/or people of color, 80 percent of leaders are women, and over half of the **board of directors** are women. Almost half of the engineering team is female—that's right, 50 percent! Jenn made waves this year when she equalized benefits—things like bereavement leave, parental leave, family sick leave, and sabbatical packages—for all employees. As she wrote in a *New York Times* opinion piece, "I had inadvertently created classes of employees—and by doing so, had done my part to contribute to America's inequality problem. . . . This has to change. As a founder of a company that has grown over the last eight years, I implicitly understand that Rent the Runway would not exist without the dedication and loyalty of our team. Don't I owe it to the team that got me here to take care of them?" Now the CEO and the warehouse workers all get the same benefits, which is practically unheard of.

Jenn and Jenny used most of their savings and bought a hundred dresses at Bloomingdale's. They bought in their own sizes, so if all else failed, at least they'd have a killer wardrobe.

Even for her 2017 wedding on a beach in the Hamptons, she made a conscious effort to elevate women. She used almost all female vendors—the DJ and her event planner, among many others, were gals. To further promote women entrepreneurs, she launched Project Entrepreneur, a competition and **incubator** previously housed inside Rent the Runway.

Jenn met her husband while doing online dating for the first time, on the app Hinge. They fell in love fast. She was thirty-four, and they both wanted kids, so after they got engaged, she got pregnant immediately. Their daughter, Aurora, at age five months, was at the wedding (of course), wearing a custom-made party dress. Unfortunately, she couldn't rent it from Rent the Runway—no toddler dresses at that point!

SARA BLAKELY

FOUNDER AND CEO OF

SPANX

Business 101: Fake it till you make it.

HER BUSINESS: Spanx makes every type of "shapewear" for under your clothes, from boy briefs to bodysuits and sports bras to arm tights, all making people feel and look dynamite.

VERY FIRST JOB: A kiddie camp. I walked the beach in my town of Clearwater, Florida, and offered parents a break from their kids. The price: $8 an hour.

AS A KID, WHAT I WANTED TO BE WHEN I GREW UP: I wanted to be a lawyer, like my dad. He would get me out of school to watch his closing arguments in court.

MY BEDTIME: Eight-thirty—but I fall asleep by ten. Sometimes we have a masseuse come. My husband is an avid runner, and he got us hooked on getting leg and foot massages.

ON MY BUCKET LIST: Travel the world and live like a local in a different place each month. For the twelfth month, spin the globe and go wherever my finger lands!

A GUILTY PLEASURE: Cheez-Its. (I'm a nervous flyer and always eat them in-flight to calm down!)

FAVORITE CHILDHOOD BOOK: The Wayne Dyer *How to Be a No-Limit Person* cassette series. I had all ten cassettes and listened over and over until I had them all memorized. Literally.

ADVICE I'D GIVE TO MY THIRTEEN-YEAR-OLD SELF: Don't invest a lot of energy or time on being upset about a boy who doesn't like you. If I could go back and take the time I invested in stressing about whether a guy did or didn't dig me, and do something more creative, more positive, that'd be something.

Sara Blakely has always had little patience for constricting, hot pantyhose that stick to her skin. Worse still are those same hose under dress pants. But when she was just starting out in business, sometimes she had to sport the dreaded combo. It was the only way she could wear her fave off-white dress pants, which she'd spent $99 on—a major splurge! Worn alone, the pants revealed terrible panty lines—definitely not professional-looking.

That all changed when she turned twenty-seven. She was out selling fax machines door-to-door to Atlanta offices. Fax salesgirl was no dream job, but she had struck out with law school (bombed the LSAT) and a roving character job at Disneyland (she didn't get cast as Goofy; they offered chipmunk). Lucky for Sara, her cool dad always promoted failure. "Fail! Fail! Fail!" he'd say. "And then go try another crazy thing." (If your dad, grandma, or even weirdo neighbor tells you to fail fast and often, do *not* roll your eyeballs—it will free you to do great things.)

While Sara was roasting one afternoon in her dress pants–pantyhose combination, an idea entered her brain. She grabbed scissors and hacked the feet and legs off her hose.

Voilà—no more claustrophobic thighs or stockinged toes showing in her sandals. She peeked in the mirror: Legs free. Lines gone. Looking good! This worked!

She was so pleased with her invention that she knew her friends would want it, too. And her friend's friends. And probably her mom and her mom's friends. And their neighbors' friends . . .

Sara, though, didn't know anything about how to replicate what she'd done. She needed to produce hefty, elastic-y, legless hose, but she didn't sew and had never worked in fashion. A quick Google search of *hosiery mills* turned up several nearby in North Carolina. She took a week off work, drove there, and started knocking on doors. The mill people all asked the same three questions: Who are you? Sara Blakely, she'd say. And you're from? Sara Blakely's company. And you're financed by? Sara Blakely. Then they'd shake their heads and the meeting was over. She returned home empty-handed. Two weeks later, though, one of the manufacturers called. His three daughters had convinced him that her idea was dynamite. He would make her crazy product.

His mill produced samples—**prototypes**—to show stores. Sara looked up department stores in the phone book to **cold-call,** which is a fully nerve-racking act of frustration and faith where you dial without knowing anyone and bumble through explaining yourself and hope someone will listen. Mostly you get hung up on, but sometimes it's the only option.

While Sara was roasting one afternoon in her dress pants–pantyhose combination, an idea entered her brain. She grabbed scissors and hacked the feet and legs off her hose.

After many nos, a Neiman Marcus buyer said if Sara would fly to Dallas, she would give her ten minutes. Sara threw her sample in her lucky red backpack and went (her friends all pleaded for her to ditch that ratty bag for a cute purse, but she refused). She was only a few minutes into pitching her invention when the vibe in the room started feeling about as vibrant as a soggy tuna sandwich. The buyer wasn't following up with a single question or comment. Nada. Refusing to blow the opportunity, Sara led the buyer into the bathroom, then ducked into a stall and pulled on her special legless hose. Twirling around, she said, "Isn't this bum *so* much better?" Clearly it was, because the buyer put in an order to stock Sara's thingamajigs. (They still needed a name!)

Sara has a habit of saying yes in the moment and then figuring out how to make whatever she's promised work. She'd found someone to make her prototype, but she didn't know who could manufacture her underthings in bulk. Or what to call them yet. Or how to package them (probably not in boring taupe boxes like every other hose packager). Still, she told Neiman Marcus "Of course!" She would figure it all out and deliver. (BTW, this is different from you saying "Of course" when your mom asks "Have you done your homework?")

Tip: Carry a pocket-sized notebook to log ideas on the go!

Sara thought up the name Spanks while driving. In fact, Sara does all her best inventing while driving. "You know Einstein invented best in the shower, while shaving. Something about the rote motion. For me it's in the car," she said. The best name she had before Spanks was Open-Toed Delilahs—yikes! She started brainstorming *k* words. Why? She thought about brands she remembered best—Nikon and Coke. Both have the *k* sound. *K*s must have powers. So *k* words . . . *k* words. Spanks! She pulled over and jotted it down. She has piles of Mead notebooks where she keeps ideas. Her assistant transfers them to a list on the computer, which is currently 109 pages of ideas! During trademarking she changed the *k*s to an *x*, because made-up words are easier to trademark, and she preserved the *k* sound.

She could barely wait for the first shipments of slim red-and-black boxes to start arriving at Neiman Marcus stores. What a fantasy! But when she popped into the closest Neiman Marcus to peek at her Spanx and see the display of bold packages, her heart sank. They were

Tip: Lean into the problem. Nothing improves by just getting sour-faced when things bomb. What could YOU do NOW to make it better?

buried deep in the hosiery aisle hinterlands—who would ever find them there? And if they sat undiscovered collecting dust, Neiman Marcus would quickly discontinue carrying them, chalk up the whole experiment as a miss, and pack the Spanx away to free up the shelf space. No! She dashed to Target, bought a cardboard rack, hid it inside her coat, and sneakily stood it at the Neiman Marcus register. Then she filled it with her Spanx. No one stopped her. Moving with such authority, she looked like she worked there!

Taking no chances, she called up elementary school pals in all the seven cities of the seven Neiman Marcuses and begged them to buy up all her Spanx. (She even promised to pay them back.)

Sara has a habit of saying yes in the moment and then figuring out how to make whatever she's promised work.

She knew she had a great idea and that **sales** were starting to prove it; soon someone might try to copy her invention if she didn't protect herself with a patent. She sought out a patent attorney who would understand her product best—a woman. But the search was a bust—there wasn't a female doing patent law in Atlanta, or even in all of Georgia. Another lawyer wanted to charge her $3,000. Since she had just $5,000 of her own money to start the business, she went to the bookstore and got a book on how to obtain a patent. She wrote all the claims herself, basically statements describing what is unique about an invention. Her mom, an artist, provided sketches, which accompanied the patent application. Sarah also trademarked the word *Spanx,* another legal process she had to teach herself. But she did it right. The word was hers.

Now Sara is the youngest self-made female billionaire ever, from selling zillions and zillions of pairs of Spanx. Her goal has always been to make customers feel great about themselves. Before Spanx, most hose and underwear (all made by men) was sized not on real women but on plastic forms. They used one size of elastic in all hose, regardless of the size of the stockings and woman. No wonder so many hose wearers barely make it back home after work before madly tugging them off and sighing holy relief!

Sara believes that her creativity is thanks to a rare quality she observed in her parents. "Neither of them cared a bit what others thought of them," she says. She also gives credit to her willingness to give herself permission to sometimes just do nothing. "The key is spending time alone." Before she married (and had four kids), she'd often spend hours just sitting on her couch, daydreaming, wondering, questioning. Her sparks often come from asking *Why have we always done it this way? Why not another way?* When Sara recently thought, *Why are tights only for legs?* it led to the creation of arm tights in cobalt, rosy pink, neon yellow, and more! What's next? Skullcaps? Footies? We shall see where her curiosity leads her.

EMMA MCILROY

COFOUNDER AND CEO OF
WILDFANG

Business 101: Study your customer like you would your heartthrob, with extensive observation and research (and maybe a little spying!).

HER BUSINESS: Clothes, mostly bought by gals, that are not boy clothes or girl clothes but rather just clothes.

VERY FIRST JOB: Bartender. I was fourteen or fifteen. It's different in Ireland.

AS A KID, WHAT I WANTED TO BE WHEN I GREW UP: Two things— I wanted to be a hundred-meter sprinter and win the Olympics, but I wasn't good at short distances. I also wanted to write and illustrate my own book, which I've done.

A WEIRD THING YOU'LL FIND ON (OR IN) MY DESK: A picture of me and my wife at Benihana.

HIGH SCHOOL GPA: I broke records for grades, so I guess 4.0.

WORST SUBJECT IN SCHOOL: History.

MY BEDTIME: Eleven p.m.

ON MY BUCKET LIST: Go to Ethiopia.

A GUILTY PLEASURE: *Guilt* is such an interesting word. I don't feel too much of it. Cadbury Chocolate, I guess.

AN EXPRESSION I USE A LOT THAT PEOPLE KNOW ME FOR: "What about ye?" It's Irish.

FAVORITE CANDY: Cadbury Caramel.

FAVORITE CHILDHOOD BOOK: *Great Expectations.*

HOW OFTEN I CHECK MY SALES: Probably once a day.

A TOOL I ALWAYS WANT TO HAVE IN MY HOUSE: I'm renovating my whole house and doing a lot of it myself. I've been needing wire cutters.

SOME WORDS TO LIVE BY: I don't give a crud (adjusted to G-rating) how you want to dress, just do you.

FAVORITE DESIGNER: Alexander Wang.

ADVICE I'D GIVE TO MY THIRTEEN-YEAR-OLD SELF: Be nice to people, because you never know what they are going through, and you are likely to come across them again.

Just hours after Melania Trump took that fateful trip to the Texas border in her green Zara jacket sloganized with *I Really Don't Care, Do U?* Emma and her creative director were photoshopping *I Really Care, Don't U?* onto a picture of a similar-looking army jacket they luckily already sold on the website. This way they could have the jacket on sale immediately even though they hadn't made it yet. Then, as quickly as possible, they got the jackets printed with the new slogan and shipped out to purchasers. They sold out within forty-five minutes. They got more jackets. Within two weeks they sold $300,000 worth and donated all that to the Refugee and Immigrant Center for Education and Legal Services (RAICES), a nonprofit providing free and low-cost legal services to immigrants and refugees.

> **Tip:** Supporting philanthropic causes is a winner all around. You did something good. Someone in need gets help. Your customers will get the warm fuzzies about you because you stand for values, not just **profit.**

No surprise, Emma lives to break rules. She welcomes hellions, rascals, and rabble-rousers (all words used in her brand messaging). She hates norms, hard-liners, and naysayers. Her mission statement includes "smashing gender roles and the patriarchy in the process." Her first store in Portland has a sign in the window: MISFITS WELCOME. Are you getting the idea? This girl is a REBEL.

Wildfang began on a shopping spree at an Urban Outfitters store. Emma was with her pal and Nike coworker Julia when she picked out a cool tee with a picture of Kate Moss emblazoned on it. Julia fell for this awesome gray blazer with elbow patches. Unfortunately, the blazer was long in the arms and too tight to button. The T-shirt hung weird. They had mistakenly ambled into the men's section because, well, the clothes they always gravitate toward are guys' clothes. "Why don't they make stuff like this for women?" Julia asked Emma. Before long, they quit their well-paying Nike jobs (Emma worked in digital sports marketing) to start a tomboy clothing brand, becoming "female Robin Hoods raiding men's closets and maniacally dispensing blazers, cardigans, wingtips, and bowlers" to give to gals. Remember Robin Hood? He hopped around with bow and arrow stealing from the rich to give to the poor.

Wildfang is the German word for "tomboy." Emma's concept is clothing that tosses out the rigid rules defining girls' apparel. They're "curating some of the raddest tomboy fashions—from wingtips to bow ties and button-downs," as the company says.

Her mission statement includes "smashing gender roles and the patriarchy in the process." Her first store in Portland has a sign in the window: MISFITS WELCOME.

Before launch, Emma wanted to check her instinct that there were plenty of women like her keen to wear guy-ish styles. She did 170 hours of consumer research, visiting forty-three gals at home in their Portland bedrooms and spending four hours going through closets, talking, and shopping online with them. She continually heard two things: They had no favorite stores, and they wanted boyish style—the look of their guy friend's shirt, or their grandfather's military jacket from the sixties, but designed to fit a female body. Within one month of opening online, 22,000 people had registered as customers and fans. Today Wildfang is a multimillion-dollar retailer.

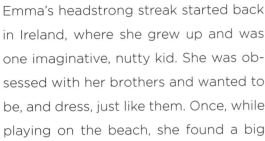

Emma's headstrong streak started back in Ireland, where she grew up and was one imaginative, nutty kid. She was obsessed with her brothers and wanted to be, and dress, just like them. Once, while playing on the beach, she found a big gray rock that she swore was a mammoth's foot. Her mom, who Emma credits with fueling her independence, didn't laugh at her discovery. She didn't squash her idea with practical questions like "How could this possibly come from an extinct animal that hasn't roamed in eons?" Instead she said, "Yeah, maybe," and suggested dropping by the local museum to have an expert look at her find. A few days later the phone rang. "It's not a mammoth's foot," the museum's paleontologist said. "It's a two-hundred-million-year-old ichthyosaur skull." Her mom's whole face lit up at the call, and yes, she was shocked. *I know better than to doubt you!* her mom's supportive smile said. Now Emma's mantra is "Yeah, maybe." She's all about imagining the best outcome instead of the worst, and remembering that magical, unlikely things do happen, and most frequently to people who are willing to suspend judgment, dream, and focus on the possible.

> **Tip:** Next time you're feeling negative and listing all the ways your idea could flop, try the opposite instead. Visualize things going exactly right. This is what soccer players do, picturing themselves making the winning goal or that critical save. Try it!

The brand quickly came to mean much more than clothing. Customers wanted to buy the tomboy looks, but they also liked the feeling of being part of a club of people who felt *Finally, someone gets me!* Their brand manifesto helped stoke this sense of belonging: "We are not a brand. We are a band." To give women a place to rub shoulders with their Wildfang sisters, Emma has opened four stores, the newest in Los Angeles, the one before that in über-hip SoHo in New York City, and two in Portland, Oregon. No surprise, their flagship store in Portland isn't like other stores. It's named Fort Wildfang. There are swings inside. Customers are asked to carve in the wood wall—because everyone should always leave their mark. They hold "Free Speech" open-mic nights.

Emma says the winner isn't the one who avoids mistakes; it's the one who quits last.

One sign that their product is hitting the mark is that trendy stores like Forever 21 are copying them. Wildfang coined the slogan "Wild Feminist" and printed it on tees, jackets, and more, and then, boom, Forever 21 had stuff printed with those two words. When initial legal action didn't quickly shut this down, Emma decided the best response was to take this as a compliment and move on. (I bet your mom has told you that imitation is the sincerest form of flattery when you are hating on your friend who just bought your same backpack/earrings/jeans.)

Emma expects failure. Mistakes, disappointments, and troubles are daily. She says the winner isn't the one who avoids mistakes; it's the one who quits last. (Katia Beauchamp at Birchbox says this, too. See page 129.) She has tactics to handle stressful moments, like an important team member quitting on her birthday, or having to find $250,000 in twenty-four hours after an investor withdrew (both true). For one, she practices visualization. She closes her eyes and pictures something calming in her mind. For her, that is Barack Obama, who she regards as exceedingly coolheaded and steady. She also forces herself to wait to respond. "I've taught myself to never reach out immediately verbally or in email. I just take info in and give myself some time."

Emma is all about being authentic. She's feminist. She's gay. She's Christian. Those three things don't often go together for people. They require having a backbone. "What a stinky feeling when you can't be yourself. I never wanted to be like everybody else. I never wanted to think like everybody else. That seemed fake, and a waste of time." Pretty powerful thinking, right?

KATRINA LAKE

FOUNDER AND CEO OF
STITCH FIX

Business 101: Reimagine something outdated and uninspired.

HER BUSINESS: A new take on a personal stylist—a subscription clothing-box service for the whole household. Stylists "dress" customers using survey data, then ship the fashions. Users keep what they love and send the rest back.

SCENES FROM WORK: One Stitch Fix fanatic called customer service and asked them to hide an engagement ring (he supplied it!) in a box going to his girlfriend. The rest is history.

CUSTOMER HABITS: The most colorful clothes are sold to Stitch Fixers in Kentucky. The least colorful picks go to Minnesotan Stitch Fixers.

WHAT SHE ATE AS A KID: Katrina's mom is Japanese and her dad is American, so as a kid, her lunch box contained sandwiches two days a week and Japanese rice balls (aka *onigiri*) on the other days.

There's a photo of Katrina Lake that went viral in 2017. She's standing poised and glamorous in a burgundy dress, holding a most unexpected accessory on her hip—her fourteen-month-old son dressed in a teeny blue blazer and hugging his stuffed cat. (When he cried, she jammed a bagel in his mouth.) It's a cute photo but hardly worth a second look unless you understand the momentous events of that day: Her company, Stitch Fix, had just joined the **stock exchange,** and she, at age thirty-four, had become the youngest solo female CEO *ever* to **take a company public.**

Going public—or joining the stock market—allows individuals and institutions to buy small pieces of your business (aka stocks), and the money earned from those stock purchases allows a company to grow quickly. No woman had ever posed for a photo quite like that before.

From the start, even before she knew which business she was entering, Katrina had her mind set on reinventing something broken. First she considered the hunting and fishing industries. She drove to New Hampshire to check out hunting and fishing outfitters, convinced she could do better. But she quickly abandoned the idea. She wasn't feeling any passion. Reinventing clothes shopping was her other idea. She felt the whole experience was in need of a remake. Who wanted to suffer picking through stuffed racks holding every size? No wonder many malls and department stores were closing. Shopping was moving online, but the experience there had its own pitfalls: it was terribly impersonal and frustrating. Who wants to buy and return, and buy and return, to find the one right item?

Very early in her career, even before business school, Katrina had a vision to create futuristic clothing stores modeled after museums. Shoppers would point a wand at their desired items on artful displays. Those picks, in the right size, also maybe a size up and a size down, would be waiting in the dressing room. The reaction to this brainstorm: "People looked at me like I had seven heads," she described on the podcast *How I Built This.*

Tip: Nothing fuels invention like personal frustration. What is peeving you right now?

With experience, her thinking evolved. She contemplated how miserable and overwhelming internet jeans shopping had become. Such an endless selection! So many tabs open on the computer in hopes of contrasting and comparing! What jumped out was the need for a personal shopper, someone offering up a small selection matching your style, colors, build, and bank account. It would be the anti-Amazon, curated *just for you.* And what if the clothes came to your house in a weekly or monthly box, but you would only buy what you liked and send back the rest?

The subscription-box concept drew many furrowed brows. At the time, it was untested. One of her Harvard business professors called her idea "an inventory nightmare." Pick perfect jeans for other people? Impossible, naysayers scoffed. "When you are doing something no one else is doing, you are either the smartest or the stupidest person in the room. For years, I didn't know which one I was," she said on *How I Built This.*

But she was confident enough to run a test. She bought a bunch of clothes from Boston boutiques, running up her credit card to its

$6,000 limit. She signed up twenty people to receive fashions chosen specifically for them. First they filled out a profile listing their favorite brands, colors they would not be caught dead wearing, style icons, measurements, and so on. She carefully noted the boutiques' return policies so she could stay within the fourteen- or thirty-day refund period for items that customers didn't want. Enough people liked her picks to encourage her to keep going.

"When you are doing something no one else is doing, you are either the smartest or the stupidest person in the room. For years, I didn't know which one I was."

Her brief stint working in a venture capital firm before business school emboldened her to start the business. While she says she was largely a glorified note taker, she did meet over one hundred entrepreneurs. "All of these people were super-unqualified normal people with lots of ideas, just like I was," she says. Her first try at a name was Rack Habit, but she worried that Nordstrom would sue her for the company sounding too much like Nordstrom Rack. So Stitch Fix, as in a regular hit or fix to satisfy your clothing addiction, it was. Initially, a cofounder helped Katrina launch Stitch Fix, but she left two years into the journey.

In the early days, when there were just a few forgiving users and lots of room to experiment, mess up, and try again, she did just that. She tried packing ten items per box. The feedback was "Whoa, too many options!" People didn't have the patience to try on all that. She learned more still, reading comments customers sent with returns. Every reject and purchase provided valuable data. If a gangly gal reported Frame jeans didn't fit, Katrina noted that similar jeans should be sent only to curvier types. She hired TaskRabbit helpers to carefully log all the survey data.

A waiting list formed for her Stitch Fix boxes. But Katrina still couldn't afford an expansive enough selection to ensure happiness with her picks among a broad and diverse group. To keep her customers happy, she would need many more clothes options to pick from, and to have that she needed investment.

If a waiting list doesn't convince investors your idea is a hot one, what will? That semester at Harvard, Katrina arranged her schedule so that all her classes were in one half of the week to accommodate trips to California to **pitch** venture capitalists for funding. She got lucky with one who quickly offered her half a million dollars. He challenged Katrina to get other investors to give the rest of the money she needed. This was in February. But thirty requests yielded thirty rejections. Some VCs worried about all the inventory she would need; others felt the business plan wasn't worked out enough. Happily, her first funder pitched in the rest, enough to launch. In May, she graduated. In June, she opened Stitch Fix HQ in some cramped downtown San Francisco digs. She hired some employees.

For a year, she played "stylist," picking clothes based on surveys and feedback. She packed boxes, or "fixes," as she called them. She was figuring her business out as she went along. The whole team devoted Mondays to the down-and-dirty task of picking and packing boxes. The numbers grew and grew. They had 29 subscribers, then 35, then 110, then 235. . . . All this happened with zero marketing. An intern at one point said to Katrina, "I'm really worried. How can Stitch Fix scale doing so much manually?" Katrina always knew this was only temporary.

Her grand concept had never been to simply rely on pencil-jotted feedback and handpicking frocks. She would eventually bring "big data" to the challenge of the

> **Tip:** Perfectionism will stifle all your momentum. Your concept is never going to feel 100 percent baked and ready. Trying things is how you get answers.

perfect-fit boyfriend jeans and flowery camisole. Just as Netflix tracks your movie likes and dislikes and matches that data with your age and address and prior picks to give you great "Watch this next" recommendations (you know it does that, right?), Katrina planned for algorithmic intelligence to take over the job of a salesperson in the store.

And that's what came to pass. Today, more than one hundred data scientists work at Stitch Fix figuring out how to tell software what fits, suits, and delights every Stitch Fixer. They track forty measurements on every men's shirt, for instance, and are becoming experts on desirable traits in clothing. Who knew cap sleeves would be such a winner? By 2018 Stitch Fix had expanded, offering clothes to men and children. They made over $1.2 billion in clothing sales.

Katrina insists that she was never supposed to be a big-shot entrepreneur. She doesn't have any "cute stories about running a lemonade stand," she told an *Elle* reporter. She wasn't always a standout, and owning a business wasn't some lifelong dream. "I'm not someone that people looked at and said, 'Oh, she's going to be a CEO.' That wasn't the path I was putting myself on," she reflected in *Elle*. In fact, she went to college at Stanford assuming she would become a doctor, like her dad.

She used to resent getting praise that revolved around her gender. "There was one point where I felt I should be [called] a tech CEO and not a woman CEO," she told *Elle*. But now she's changed her tune. She recognizes that she is playing an important pioneering role and that calling that out will help women behind her move ahead. She never wants to get so high and mighty that she forgets what got her to this point. As CEO, she says she still works in the trenches, choosing fashions for five of the "fixes" to be sent out each week.

FOOD

NATASHA CASE

COFOUNDER AND CEO OF
COOLHAUS

Business 101: Combine two of your passions for a really zany, mega-original business idea. Architects and ice cream, anyone? Waffles and haircuts? The sky's the limit on what you can put together to wow customers!

HER BUSINESS: Delish ice cream in wacky flavors. Available nationwide at grocery stores and in a few Coolhaus stores and trendy trucks.

A WEIRD THING YOU'LL FIND ON (OR IN) MY DESK: A little sculpture that looks like a melting Popsicle, signed by the artist, which I got at the Museum of Ice Cream.

HIGH SCHOOL GPA: High 3s. I took a lot of APs, so could be around a 4.0.

WORST SUBJECT IN SCHOOL: I loved physics but was not into chemistry.

VERY FIRST JOB: A ball girl for UCLA basketball games. I'd make like fifteen dollars per game, which was hugely exciting. I had to open a bank account for my checks.

AS A KID, WHAT I WANTED TO BE WHEN I GREW UP: I wanted to be in sports medicine.

MY BEDTIME: Between ten-thirty and eleven-thirty. My son always wakes up at seven-thirty a.m.

ON MY BUCKET LIST: I really want to check out India and Thailand and go back to Japan with my family. And I want to make Coolhaus a $100 million company and beyond.

A GUILTY PLEASURE: Dirty martinis (my wife is coming out with a new gin).

FAVORITE CANDY: Probably peanut M&M's.

FAVORITE CHILDHOOD BOOK: *The Voice of the Wood.* It's about an instrument maker who makes a special cello.

HOW OFTEN I CHECK MY BANK STATEMENT: With every transaction, I get an email. I'm very, very into [knowing the numbers]. I also get a daily report.

A TOOL I ALWAYS WANT TO HAVE IN MY HOUSE: A great blender and a really good strainer. And a great cocktail setup.

How do chicken skins cooked in caramel sound? Natasha is a huge fan, because that's the secret to Coolhaus's amazing Fried Chicken and Waffles ice cream. She sprinkles in some cayenne and sage for added savory deliciousness. Devising far-out flavors that involve weird combos of ingredients and somehow come out tasting like they were meant to be together is Natasha's superpower. Some of her seventy most popping flavors: Froot Loops Cereal Milk, Jewish Deli, Spiked

Coffee & Donuts, and Avocado Sea Salt. What will she think of next? Her flavor philosophy: "You want to hit on nostalgia but also do something new. That's the name of the game."

Tip: A trade secret is a recipe, process, or special invention that a company guards like crown jewels because otherwise competitors might copy it! Mars, the maker of Snickers, famously guards secrets. Contractors repairing candy-making machinery reportedly used to be led through Mars factories blindfolded.

Natasha had to modify her industrial ice cream machines to accommodate her unique mixtures. Available machines can take one swirl-in (like chocolate ribbons) and one mix-in (like Heath bars). To make a batch of Buttered French Toast ice cream, she adds two mix-ins—buttered-toast pieces and candied pecans—plus a maple swirl. Her Milkshake and Fries flavor, which is so popular they couldn't keep it in the store for two years running, also takes two mix-ins. She tosses in something kind of like shoestring potatoes and homemade candy malt balls. She won't reveal what she uses for the fries, because that is a **trade secret**! The Milkshake and Fries combo came about when Natasha noticed people around town happily dipping their fries into their shakes. "I love the idea of taking this subversive act people do at Wendy's and In-N-Out all the time, and celebrating that genius move," she explains.

One of Natasha's top sellers happened by accident. Dirty Mint Chip looks "dirty" because she added brown sugar when she ran out of white sugar. That night she was also feeling lazy, so she skipped straining out the mint leaves. Voilà—Dirty Mint Chip.

The great ice cream adventure started back in 2008, when Natasha was working in architecture at Disney. The economy was tanking, and lots of **layoffs** were happening. To cheer up her coworkers, Natasha would make them ice cream sandwiches.

She would tweak and tweak her cookie recipes, Goldilocks-style. Not too bendy. Not too crumbly. But *juuuuust* right! To an architect, two cookies with a creamy center resembled a "cool house"—thus the name Coolhaus. It's also a nod to Bauhaus, a modern design movement of the 1920s and '30s.

A killer idea she had was edible wrappers for her ice cream sandwiches.

Around this time, Natasha met Freya, who became her girlfriend (and later her wife) and business partner. The pair egged each other on to make ice cream their work. They had a cool idea for how to launch. They trolled Craigslist and found a twenty-year-old mail truck converted into a food truck. They plopped down $2,500, and it was theirs. Never mind that the truck didn't have a working engine. Their brilliant thought was to introduce Coolhaus at the ultra-hipster music fest Coachella, which happens every spring in the desert outside Los Angeles. The morning of the festival, they called up AAA road service, where they were members, and told them their engine was dead and they needed a tow. (Remember, it wasn't really dead—it had never worked!) They'd read that every AAA customer gets one free tow, up to two hundred miles. Boom—this was their ticket to getting their store on wheels to Coachella.

Parked there, they scooped enough of their clever architect-honoring ice cream flavors to prove to themselves that they had a hot idea. Clearly customers appreciated Mies Vanilla Rohe, after Ludwig Mies van der Rohe, who helped define modern architecture, and Frank Berry, for Los Angeles–based Frank Gehry, who designed the funky Walt Disney Concert Hall. Within six weeks, Natasha quit her day job at Disney.

For the first two years, they got by using $5,000 of their savings, plus all their ice cream earnings. In 2011, they raised $1 million from an angel investor. They used that cash to expand beyond trucks and into grocery stores. Their first grocery store was Whole Foods. Natasha says getting stocked there was more straightforward than people imagine. "I think people have a lot of build-up about getting into grocery stores. I literally just showed up. I found someone near the

> **Tip:** Angel investors are funders of very early-stage businesses—they save the day with their dollars!

freezer section and asked, 'How do I get my ice cream in here?'" That guy introduced her to someone with the title "head of foraging," and she made it happen. Natasha's advice: "You just have to go there and talk to people." Right now, she has two stores in Los Angeles, and food trucks in Dallas, New York, and Los Angeles. Coolhaus sold about $13 million worth of frozen deliciousness in 2018.

Of course, there have been days when they might as well be pulling out their fingernails. Natasha and Freya struggled as business partners, and ultimately Freya resigned (though they are still super in love, and now make up a threesome with their cutie son, Remy). Their expansion into Miami was a bust—their trucks were robbed and their employees were difficult—so they left town. Letting people go is one of the hardest parts of Natasha's job. "Sometimes it's the best thing for everyone, but it's never easy," she says.

Letting people go is one
of the hardest parts of Natasha's job.

As Coolhaus grew, they transitioned from hand-cranking the ice cream themselves to partnering with a manufacturer, called a co-packer. Now Natasha works with her manufacturer to figure out how the flavors get made. Perfecting her whimsical blends of savory offsetting sweet, crunchy meeting smooth, and gourmet alongside junk food is her heaven. "Who wouldn't love that? It's like a childhood dream come true!" she says. She also loves everything related to branding and design and new inventions. A killer idea she had was edible wrappers for her ice cream sandwiches. They're made of potato, with a vegetable-based ink. "When you're done, you just pop it in your mouth," she says. No muss, no fuss.

Natasha's goal (for now) is to hit $100 million in sales as a national brand that everyone gushes over. That requires always figuring out the cool new thing. "You don't want to be following. You want to predict the next wave." Coolhaus is betting on their brand-new vegan pints, including Nutella flavor—YUMMERS! Her advice is to think really big. "Women are too averse to risk. As women get more comfortable with risk, that's going to help them go for it, and raise money, and all the rest," she says. She considers Coolhaus the Ben & Jerry's of the millennial generation, just like "[our parents] had Woodstock [that hippy-filled 1960s music fest], and we have Coachella," she says. Having Hollywood celebs tout your brand, follow you on social media, and hire your trucks sure helps, too. Members of the Coolhaus fan club: Justin Bieber, Brad Pitt, and Angelina Jolie.

DIANE CAMPBELL

FOUNDER AND OWNER OF
THE CANDY STORE

Business 101: Moneymaking is not the sole sweet measure of success.

HER BUSINESS: A one-of-a-kind, beloved candy shop in San Francisco known for its inventive selections, from banana-licorice penguins to sour pineapple skulls.

VERY FIRST JOB: Selling candy on the playground.

HIGH SCHOOL GPA: I think 2.0. Is 2.0 a C? C, yeah.

A WEIRD THING YOU'LL FIND ON (OR IN) MY DESK: I have a pet tortoise (Rudy) and collect lots of tortoise things.

AS A KID, WHAT I WANTED TO BE WHEN I GREW UP: Even by age nine, I already knew I wanted to work with candy.

WORST SUBJECT IN SCHOOL: Math.

ON MY BUCKET LIST: My own radio talk show.

AN EXPRESSION I USE A LOT THAT PEOPLE KNOW ME FOR: "$%#@!" (Not kid-friendly, sorry!) Or "Oh man" or "Oy vey."

FAVORITE CANDY IN THE SHOP: Frozen vanilla Charleston Chews and Mallo Cups.

FAVORITE CHILDHOOD BOOK: *Nothing's Fair in Fifth Grade* or *Where the Sidewalk Ends.* I read those Silverstein poems to Henry [my son] every day.

HOW OFTEN I CHECK MY BANK STATEMENT: At least once a week. I know what's going on with sales because I'm seeing the transactions in the store. But that's how often I total them in our accounting books.

A TOOL I ALWAYS WANT TO HAVE IN MY HOUSE: A really good chef's knife.

ADVICE I'D GIVE TO MY THIRTEEN-YEAR-OLD SELF: The cool kids aren't so cool at forty, and the outcasts are supercool, so hang out with a few outcasts.

———

At age nine, Diane would jump on her bike and pedal furiously to the grocery store in Great Neck, New York, to buy as many big bags of Tootsie Pops and Blow Pops, Bazooka gum and Jolly Ranchers as she could for ten dollars (without telling her parents, of course). Then she would sneak her ill-gotten gains upstairs and behind her bedroom door, dial up her schoolmates, and take their "orders." She would package their selections into little sandwich bags and exchange the loot for money on the playground. "It was so easy," she says. "Every ten dollars would turn into fifty dollars." She claims that the money per item she made back then is more than she makes now on her candy delectables.

———

Selling candy as a kid was thrilling for two reasons. Most of all, because she was being *sneaky*. Her parents were health-food nuts. No delish chocolate-coated Häagen-Dazs bars in their freezer. A "treat" was a frozen yogurt bar—"not vanilla, just plain," she emphasizes.

She also loved her contraband candy store because it meant having her own money, which meant freedom. She made so much she bought herself a VCR (a machine to play movies off tapes, in the olden days before Netflix and Showtime On Demand). She bought the clothes she liked. "No more mom ranting, 'You don't need this,'" she says, laughing. And her parents noticed that she was suddenly flush. By then, word had reached them that their daughter's unauthorized play-ground candy business was booming. And, points for her dad, he was so proud of her he started helping.

Her parents were health-food nuts. No delish chocolate-coated Häagen-Dazs bars in their freezer. A "treat" was a frozen yogurt bar—"not vanilla, just plain."

There was a little candy store in her town where she went almost every Saturday for her personal stash. It was called the Candy Store. No, it is not a coincidence that her business has the same name. She had so many fond memories of ordering up her standard quarter pound of watermelon sours and quarter pound of Zagnuts (peanut buttery chunks rolled in toasted coconut) that, in time, she would name her San Francisco shop after it. The Great Neck store closed in the eight-ies, sadly, so in essence, she is keeping the spirit alive.

Diane has carefully selected every item in every jar in her store. Most of her inventory comes from tiny family businesses that make their candy in small batches, like the black and red licorice Scottie dogs that come from a secret purveyor.

(Shhhh . . . she doesn't tell anyone who makes them, because that's a trade secret and requires circling the globe—literally—to unearth the absolute most unique, tasty, and amazing treats.)

Today she has ninety-three jars on her candy wall, which extends the full length of the store's interior and holds about half of the shop's goodies. The wall—three shelves high—is her pride and joy, a visual firework, with jars of colorful balls, laces, and chunks, car- and butterfly-shaped gummies screaming to be eaten. She had the wall unit custom-built to her exact specs and made the builder confirm it could handle the weight of all that sugar, which he did by hanging from each shelf.

Before opening her shop, Diane had lots of different jobs. She was a line cook in a swank brasserie. She worked in internet marketing, even though she insists she faked her way into that job, knowing nothing about the subject. She is so outgoing and likable she can convince anyone to hire her, and then she

learns *fast*. But all her non-candy jobs left her feeling blah, especially when she got home at night and looked back at how she'd spent the day. The jobs were kind of boring. Her bosses were mediocre. She just hated having a boss, preferring to make her own rules (remember back in childhood—she made her own rules then, too). So she started asking: *What could I do that would feel meaningful, and in a place where I would be in charge?*

She had always wanted a candy store. But where to put it? And how to start? Diane sat on the corner in her choice San Francisco neighborhoods with a little hardware-store clicker, counting the foot traffic. Once she decided on the quaint Russian Hill neighborhood, no realtor would rent her a commercial space because she didn't have a business. But she couldn't start her business because she didn't have a shop. (Ever hear of a "chicken or the egg" problem?) Same issue with getting a loan. No bank wanted to give her money because she was unproven in business. She still feels forever grateful to Wells Fargo bank for loaning her $70,000. The loan "terms" (in bankspeak), or agreement, stated that she had to repay the money within seven years. Her shop was so successful she paid the loan back in one year. Ka-ching!

The most important step in launching was her business plan (see page 278 for a sample plan). "I can't overstate the importance of this," she says. "It's about thinking it through. How will we do this? Where do we want to be in three years? In five years? Are we on plan, and if not, how do we get back on?" Early on, she took any small-business class she could find. She started with a few events and a cart. She swears that she could never have succeeded without the help of her husband, Brian. He does the ordering. He even took candy-making classes, and his homemade brittles and toffees instantly became the shop's top sellers.

Her shop was so successful she paid the loan back in one year. Ka-ching!

Another bestselling item is black licorice; Diane stocks twenty different varieties. Some are gooey, others hard as rocks; some are salty, some sweet; one is even banana flavored! Almost all of it she buys in Holland. Besides licorice, she has many exotic items, like toffee pistachios, gummy chicken feet (really!), French nougat olives, and jars of Marshmallow Fluff.

In 2012, an executive at Target called out of the blue to congratulate her that hers was one of five businesses chosen to be a pop-up inside Target. Foot traffic galore. Her choice candy picks in the Candy Store-branded packaging were featured in two thousand Target stores nationwide. At a launch party she met Martha Stewart, who later visited and bought raspberry chews and artisanal dark chocolate bars, and afterward raved on her blog about "a tiny shop filled with the best candies of the world!"

Diane has a golden rule in the shop. A candy store should be a fantasyland. A place where you walk in and feel like you might be in a dream.

She wants every customer sense tingling, total excitement. Cliché, yes, but you should feel like a kid in a candy store! That means rules like "Never let anyone see you refilling the candy jars from a big plastic bag of stock. Seeing that breaks the spell of wonder and fantasy," Diane says. "Preserve the magic at all costs!"

KARA GOLDIN

FOUNDER AND CEO OF

HINT

Business 101: Selling better health is always a smart bet.

HER BUSINESS: Delish, fruity-tasting bottled water made from fruit oils, with zero chemicals or calories. Just added: fruity sunscreen that is oxybenzone-free (bad chemical) and fruity (of course)!

A WEIRD THING YOU'LL FIND ON (OR IN) MY DESK: A pad of paper. When I really have to remember something, I write it on paper and stuff it in my back pocket.

ON MY BUCKET LIST: Visiting Africa.

A GUILTY PLEASURE: Thai massage on Sundays.

FAVORITE CHILDHOOD BOOK: *James and the Giant Peach.*

DRIVES ME CRAZY: Disorganization.

WORKING ON MASTERING: Me time.

WORST PART OF MY JOB: Firing people.

BEST PART OF MY JOB: Developing products and breaking norms in the process.

ADVICE I'D GIVE TO MY THIRTEEN-YEAR-OLD SELF: You are smart enough to figure it out.

Of course everyone asks Kara which Hint water flavor is her favorite, and she always gives the same answer: "That's like asking me to choose my favorite child." When pressed she picks pineapple. She likes flat water in the morning and fizzy in the afternoon—Hint makes both. She estimates she drinks about eighty bottles of Hint water a week, and sometimes as many as one hundred. At home, she has a fully stocked fridge. Kara and her family live right off a hiking trail, and close friends all know the gate code and come in and help themselves.

Kara still can't believe she works in the beverage industry. She worked in tech forever, most recently as the youngest VP at internet service provider AOL, growing shopping partnerships into a $1 billion business. That was after graduating from Arizona State University and a stint in New York City to work in media. So why water?

It all began with a personal problem. Kara had about fifty pounds of baby weight on her after birthing three kids, and she just couldn't seem to shed it. She was drowning in ten to twelve cans of Diet Coke daily. And although they helped cut her snacking, she realized the alternative was worse—the chemicals listed on the side of the can read like something she should put in her car engine, Kara said. She had a revelation that she needed to go clean. Plus, she wasn't losing weight anyway. She needed a health kick, and rule number one is always: Drink more water. Problem was, she hated boring, tasteless water.

Tip: If you make something that you can't keep around because everyone who comes through is snarfing it, you are sitting on a winning idea. Get on it!

She started fiddling with livening up her water by plopping in chunks of fruit. Soon she was boiling fruits to extract their oils and using them to get a fruity taste without pulp or sugar. (Beware: "One time I forgot about it, boiled it to nothing . . . and my stove caught on fire.") When she did it right, her concoction was surprisingly tasty. The fruity water became her new habit. When she left a batch in the fridge, her kids and husband guzzled it. Her pounds started melting away, and a business idea fizzed up.

She decided to bottle some and try to sell it. At her San Francisco Whole Foods, she casually asked a worker stocking shelves what it takes to get a drink into the store inventory. "Do you have experience in the beverage industry?" he asked. No. "You have food experience, then?" No. But she was so persistent that he told her to bring in some Hint water if she ever got it properly bottled.

She has a long list of things she was clueless about when she began trying to manufacture Hint. She was searching for a "bottler" but learned that drink makers and bottlers are called co-packers. She learned that drinks need to have a long shelf life so they can sit a long time without spoiling. Everyone insisted the only way to ensure a long shelf life was to add preservatives. But her point in making Hint was to keep chemicals OUT. With some digging, she discovered a heating process that acted like a preservative. Bingo.

She needed a health kick, and rule number one is always: Drink more water. Problem was, she hated boring, tasteless water.

Now she had to go find her Whole Foods friend. The day her first ten store-ready cases arrived on her doorstep was also the day she was supposed to give birth to her fourth child. But she was going to make time for both, darn it! At ten a.m., she was rushing her cases into Whole Foods. Her shelf-stocker pal was standing by and kept his word. He took her number and said he'd let her know how they sold. She wasn't even home from the hospital with her newborn when the phone rang. It was Whole Foods calling to report that the ten cases were gone. "Wait, who took them?" she asked. The insta-sellout was so unexpected she thought they'd been stolen.

Her Whole Foods story is a fairy tale, but it's not an indication of how Hint's launch went everywhere. "I had more failure in the first year than I had in the five years of my career prior," Kara says. One killer rejection: She was happily selling Hint water in some 11,000 Starbucks when then-CEO Howard Schultz decided he wanted fewer drinks and more food in his edibles case. Starbucks suddenly canceled the Hint order, leaving Kara with enough blackberry Hint to drown a small nation.

What happened next speaks to Kara's belief that you can't have a rainbow without a few (or a lot of) rain showers. A blackberry-Hint-loving guy who worked for Amazon called soon after the Starbucks cancellation. He had bumped into blackberry Hint in Starbucks, loved it, and wondered: Could he put in a huge order for Amazon's new grocery delivery service? Kara is certain he would never have tried Hint had it not been in Starbucks, however briefly.

One of her best ideas since launching is offering Hint water directly to people through a subscription service. A case is sent to the subscriber's home at regular intervals so the household is never short on Hint. She has even gotten Hint onto many college campuses. These days, Hint water has over $90 million in sales. One phenomenon Kara can be proud of is "Hint hoarding." At Google headquarters, employees started stashing their fave flavors under their desks. The techies are a loyal fan base. All over **Silicon Valley,** from Facebook to Slack to Airbnb, employees are guzzling Hint. Kara created Hint Kick, a caffeinated version, with them in mind, to get them off sugar-loaded Red Bull and Monster Energy.

But that isn't to say Hint doesn't have competition. Kara never knew that Coke and Pepsi pay grocery chains tens of millions of dollars for prime shelf space. **Start-ups** can't compete with that. LaCroix sparkling water recently resurged as an unlikely sensation. Her competitive edge, she says, is clean bottling. LaCroix's aluminum cans contain BPA, a proven harmful chemical. But there are others encroaching:

> **Tip:** Figure out how to get your product into the hands of buzz creators, tastemakers, celebs (aim high, right?). Not all customers are created equal for turning your brand cool.

Pepsi's flavored sparkling water Bubly and Coca-Cola's sugar-enhanced Vitaminwater. Kara's got a competitive takedown for all of them. Exhibit A: "I thought vitamins weren't supposed to have sugar."

It was Whole Foods calling to report that the ten cases were gone. "Wait, who took them?" she asked. The insta-sellout was so unexpected she thought they'd been stolen.

But better health doesn't only have to do with what you drink. Kara is fair skinned and spent her childhood in the Arizona sun, which is key to the second act of Hint's story. A blotch on her nose turned out to be early-stage skin cancer. She dived into sunscreen science. She was applying sunscreen religiously, but the splotch kept growing. Now she wondered—much like during her 2005 light-bulb moment that had her inspecting the unpronounceable ingredients on a Diet Coke can—*What exactly is in this cream I'm using?* Reading a few studies, she discovered that an ingredient in 90 percent of sunscreens, oxybenzone, may affect bodily hormones, and some cancers are linked to hormones.

The same way she took to her kitchen to boil fruit to improve water, Kara began working to improve sunscreen. Bugged that the teeny tube recommended by her doc was priced like liquid gold, she ordered all the ingredients listed on the back of the tube. She started concocting and exploring ways to make it cheaper and safer. Then she had a brain zing: Why not also make it original and very

Hint? Add some fruit oil—right? Her sunscreen avoided oxybenzone and smelled like pineapple and pear! It was affordable. In late 2017, she received approval for her new product from the **FDA** (Food and Drug Administration), and within months she launched in 1,200 Target stores nationwide.

Hint now stands for only good things in and on your body. There will be more products. Kara will continue advocating for health and less trickery in marketing. She lobbies Congress. She's on a MISSION!

SCIENCE

ANNE WOJCICKI

COFOUNDER AND CEO OF
23ANDME

Business 101: Even major, almost-company-ending setbacks can be overcome.

HER BUSINESS: A personal DNA-testing company that allows people to learn about their genetics and ancestry, like what percentage East Asian they are, their risk level for blood clots, and whether they carry the gene for cystic fibrosis. The data gathered about millions of individuals is also used to develop drugs and to understand health and disease.

VERY FIRST JOB: At Edwards Luggage at Stanford Shopping Center. I was a gift wrapper mostly. I learned many important lessons, like whether to splurge for lunch in the mall or bring my lunch and save.

AS A KID, WHAT I WANTED TO BE WHEN I GREW UP: I just wanted to be financially independent.

A WEIRD THING YOU'D FIND ON (OR IN) MY DESK: Twenty bars of chocolate—all dark, weird, and from around the world. I'm always hungry!

HIGH SCHOOL GPA: I occasionally got Bs in math.

WORST SUBJECT IN SCHOOL: I liked school.

MY BEDTIME: Ten p.m.

ON MY BUCKET LIST: Travel to Antarctica with my kids.

A GUILTY PLEASURE: Sitting around all day doing nothing.

FAVORITE CHILDHOOD BOOK: *The Great Gatsby.*

ADVICE I'D GIVE TO MY THIRTEEN-YEAR-OLD SELF: You can always take more risk. The beauty of being a kid is you can get away with it!

Anne loves making people spit. In fact, she loves it so much she holds "spit parties," passing out little vials to all attendees. Once, right in the middle of New York Fashion Week, she hosted a party and had celebrities spit in test tubes while they nibbled on fancy cheeses on crackers. Anne's company, 23andMe, which she founded with a biologist and seasoned businessperson in 2006, then processes the saliva, mining from it little bits of DNA from cells in the mouth, which are then analyzed on a tiny diagnostic chip. The spit parties are a crafty way to get attention from the press.

Tip: Stunts like spit parties, or Lululemon offering the first thirty customers who arrive naked a free item, or the convenience store 7-Eleven giving out free Slurpees on July 11 (7/11—get it?) attract attention, which draws news coverage, which drives sales! Be creative! What stunt can you dream up?

The 23andMe product is an at-home kit for collecting your own saliva. At the company, the spit then goes into a sequencing machine to read your DNA, giving you access to your genetic code. You probably learned about DNA in science class, a helix (or coil) of two twisted strands made up of a string of chemical building blocks in all different combinations. The order, which is unique in every person, is the set of instructions for *you*. Your genetic code. So 23andMe is unlocking access to your personal set of instructions. Not every building block is understood yet—not even close! But there are many things to learn from your unique code, and more discoveries about specific genes happening every day.

Your genetic code determines whether your pee smells funky after eating asparagus, whether your hair is curly or straight, and whether you can curl your tongue. (Can you?) Genes determine risk for diseases like breast cancer, cystic fibrosis, Parkinson's disease, and sickle cell anemia. Anne's big idea with 23andMe is giving people control over their own health information. Oprah called Anne's personal genetics test the ultimate selfie. True, huh?

Anne is always saying she wants to make everyone a scientist. About two months after sending off some spit, you get a super-detailed report. You learn where your ancestors *waaaaaay* back lived, and maybe that you are mostly East Asian but, surprise, also 0.2 percent Iberian and 4.5 percent West African. It might reveal you have a fourth cousin you have never heard of who lives nearby. You shared a great-great-great-grandmother, which is known based on the percentage of common DNA between you. (This can only be uncovered if you both do a 23andMe test and both make your data available.) You might learn that your genes predispose you to be extra sensitive to caffeine, or to process medicine very quickly. Some findings can be put to immediate use, at least to some degree. If you carry a known mutation that shows up in many people with celiac disease, you might begin rigorous screening or consult a doctor. Anne learned that she's at risk for breast cancer, so she basically quit alcohol because some studies suggest drinking raises your vulnerability.

Oprah called Anne's personal genetics test the ultimate selfie. True, huh?

Her idea to give us access to our DNA is very cutting-edge. She was crowned the Most Daring CEO by *Fast Company.* In 2008, her DNA test was *Time* magazine's Invention of the Year. All amazing. But don't for a minute think that her path has been smooth sailing, paved in Nutella and whipped cream. She has faced what would cause many entrepreneurs to just wilt and retreat. She was married to the CEO of Google, and they had a very public breakup. Her company was cruising along until the FDA, which regulates drugs and health tests, deemed her 254 DNA health-related tests an "unapproved medical device" with too little proven reliability, and demanded that the company cease selling. What if people acted on inaccurate results—say, had surgery they might not need? At that moment, she leaned on her mom's constant advice: Put one foot in front of the other and just *keep going.*

Her mom is clearly wise. Anne, who at first snarled back at the FDA, checked herself. Small step. She worked closely with the regulatory agency to address its concerns, some about what 23andMe promised customers in its marketing efforts. (The FDA hated the company's big TV marketing campaign.) Another step. One test was allowed to be offered again. Then ten tests, for the best-understood DNA mutations. In 2019, they added an eleventh test, for type 2 diabetes.

It's hardly surprising Anne's mom just published a fat advice book on how to raise unusually confident girls. Anne is one of three sisters. Her oldest sister, Susan, is CEO of YouTube. Her middle sister, Janet, is a smarty-pants professor in the health field. When the three were little, they were all go-getters. They were called the lemon girls because they picked lemons from their neighbors' trees and sold them up and down the street. Their dad pushed independent thinking. In fact, he was a big-deal Stanford University physicist who was trying to challenge some of Einstein's theories! That independent-thinking message stuck with his girls.

These days Anne calls herself a control freak. "One of the very hardest things for me is letting go, turning it over," she said. At work, she is trying to spend her time on things that only she can do—like giving talks or book interviews! She admits it's easy for her to fall down a rabbit hole and spend four hours formatting a presentation. "It drives me crazy if something isn't exactly centered," she says, laughing. She saves time by working while biking. "I can voice text while riding. I even wrote a whole presentation that way." She bikes to work, in her daily uniform of Lululemon running shorts and tanks. Seriously, she wears that to work pretty much every day!

As a girl, Anne did figure skating. Then she switched to ice hockey, which she played in college at Yale. She was also on a synchronized ice-skating team, a whole bunch of skaters doing dance moves at the exact same time. Being a CEO reminds her of the awesomeness of skating in unison. The role is getting the whole company working together in a beautiful dance. She loves being the CEO. "You can make decisions and execute," she says. "It's like synchronized skating [in overdrive]."

Anne has always believed in 23andMe. This is key, because her idea is so out-there that many people say she's overly optimistic. Today the company boasts five million customers. Early on, there were days when they sold fifteen or twenty kits, meaning fifteen or twenty customers. But she didn't think, *We are selling* only *fifteen or twenty.* She thought, *Wow, we are already selling fifteen to twenty!* Her view has always been that slow, steady, and positive wins the race. This just came true. In 2017, the FDA reversed its decision, approving her genetic kits. On sale again!

But don't for a minute think that her path has been smooth sailing, paved in Nutella and whipped cream. She has faced what would cause many entrepreneurs to just wilt and retreat.

The gene information uncovered by her tests does raise some difficult ethical questions. Anne has said she would be happy to know the truth about her health, good and bad, because that way she can prepare, but her matter-of-factness isn't shared by all. Kids sometimes learn that their dad is not genetically their dad. Or if one sister in a family learns she is at high risk for breast cancer, then her sisters have learned something they might rather not know, because breast cancer genes can run in families.

Anne embraces having information—the fascinating, the sad, the tricky. "We all have stories. We really impact people's sense of identity," she says. She thinks we should not shy away from information. Some mind-blowing life lessons have come from her kits. Two Minneapolis women just learned they were switched at birth, raised by the wrong parents (born thirty minutes apart on December 19, 1945, at Bethesda Hospital in Saint Paul). "We could make a hundred movies of the remarkable stories we've heard."

RACHEL HAURWITZ

COFOUNDER, PRESIDENT, AND CEO OF
CARIBOU BIOSCIENCES

Business 101: Attack the truly most challenging world problems.

HER BUSINESS: A biotech company using gene-editing technology to fight human diseases, including blood disorders and cancer, and to improve animal health and agriculture.

A WEIRD THING YOU'D FIND ON (OR IN) MY DESK: A framed picture of piglets. They are our gene-edited piglets.

MY BEDTIME: Midnight. Used to be one or two a.m. I'm trying to be on a more functional schedule.

WORST SUBJECT IN SCHOOL: Organic chemistry. I got a C.

ON MY BUCKET LIST: Visiting Africa.

A GUILTY PLEASURE: Watching football. Knowing about the neurological impact now is where the guilt comes in.

FAVORITE CANDY: Lindt chocolate.

FAVORITE CHILDHOOD BOOK: Maybe not favorite, but impactful—*The Scarlet Letter.*

ADVICE I'D GIVE TO MY THIRTEEN-YEAR-OLD SELF: Nothing in life is a straight line. Stay open to opportunities.

Rachel was already on the cutting edge of science at age fourteen. Picture this: She's at home in Austin, Texas, working on her biology assignment, which is to pick any theory and design an experiment to test it. She's read that one worm can gain another worm's memories by eating it. Boom! This was the perfect mix of weird and unbelievable. She ordered two hundred little flatworms called planaria. (The two hundred didn't come, so she purchased two hundred more, and then OF COURSE all four hundred came and she was drowning in li'l buggers!) She chose planaria because they are cannibals, meaning they eat their own kind. Now she just had to figure out how to test whether memories were transferred to the eater from the eaten.

Tip: Theories must be tested. Think a certain street corner is ideal for your slime sale? Don't just guess—test. Stand out at selling time and count the passersby. Same goes before ordering Day-Glo fabric for one hundred tube tops. Survey target wearers first.

Here's where she showed her brilliance: She divided her wormies into two groups. The first half she kept in little paper cups on her dining table. The second half she trained to go through a maze cut into a block of Styrofoam. She put worm food along the path she wanted them to take, and shot little electric jolts using a battery along the path she didn't want them to take. Once the first set of worms learned the maze, she fed them to the untrained bunch. If the theory held, the idle worms would now be maze wizzes, having absorbed the memories of where to go. The result? "Inconclusive," Rachel says. Nothing statistically meaningful. "The mystery persists!"

Here are three very cool things about her job:
(1) Every work day is completely different,
so no routine = never, ever boring!
(2) She is working on new treatments for cancer
and blood diseases.
(3) She can wear jeans to work.

But the test sure was fun and proved that she was destined to be a scientist, challenging untested facts and unlocking the hidden mysteries of creatures big and small. Her science "crush" turned true love in middle school after accompanying her dad to the Marine Biological Laboratory in Woods Hole, Massachusetts, one summer. She spent her days running around the labs there, sticking her hands in the tanks to touch starfish and live sponges.

Now she heads Caribou Biosciences, a pioneering biotech company. Here are three very cool things about her job: (1) Every work day is completely different, so no routine = never, ever boring! (2) She is working on new treatments for cancer and blood diseases. (3) She can wear jeans to work.

Here are three tricky things about her job: (1) She's often the only woman in a room full of men. (2) The groundbreaking method Caribou uses for editing genes is still relatively new, with intricacies still not understood, which demands patience and dealing with failure. (3) She is traveling constantly (about 125,000 airplane miles last year), so she's not sure she could have kids while working as she does currently. "The way I choose to spend my time now is not compatible with keeping small humans alive," she says.

So what the heck does Caribou actually make? Caribou uses CRISPR technology (pronounced how you probably want your French fries: *crisp-er*) to edit genes. CRISPR was invented by a bunch of people, but a scientist named Jennifer Doudna, who mentored Rachel and cofounded Caribou, is often credited with harnessing it. With CRISPR, an enzyme called Cas9 acts as a pair of "molecular scissors." At Caribou, a team programs little strands to take the molecular scissors to the spot that requires repair. The cut causes the cell "to go a little crazy," Rachel says, "because it wants to keep its DNA together." But eventually, a few genes fall away, and the cell is now edited, meaning whatever malfunction it had before is now fixed. So if someone has sickle cell anemia—a genetic disease—a CRISPR-based medicine can hypothetically replace the faulty gene with the correct one. Substituting genes to cure disease in humans as a routine procedure is a long way off, but Caribou is doing trials to learn enough to get there. "I would say it's in its infancy right now," Rachel says.

Rachel calls what she's doing "Microsoft Word for the genome. You can delete a paragraph or insert a sentence," she explains. There is a lot of hope this technology will someday produce monumental cures. CRISPR is so important and exciting J. Lo is even producing a TV drama series based on people using the technology.

"I'm not sure if I face more discrimination because of my age or my gender."

Rachel is running other projects, including one to engineer heartier corn and one to create healthier pigs and cows. (Remember the piglets pic on Rachel's desk? Those piglets are the result of this project.) If she succeeds, there will be a lot of happy farmers on the planet.

The field of biotechnology is notoriously male. "I'm not sure if I face more discrimination because of my age or my gender," Rachel says. One way she manages her environment is with a great poker face.

> **Tip:** Work on your poker face. Being able to disguise what you are really feeling in the moment helps in negotiations and when you are feeling unsure.

(In cards, this means not revealing if you have a good or bad hand when others are placing bets. In business, this means masking your insecurities.) Luckily, she loves poker and messing around with her face to mis-signal. "I'm fine just to be the ditzy girl everybody thinks I am, and then to walk away with all their money. I'm very comfortable with being underestimated. You can knock it out of the park while everyone is looking the other way," she says.

NINA TANDON

COFOUNDER AND CEO OF
EPIBONE

Business 101: Real breakthroughs take real time.
Have real patience.

HER BUSINESS: Growing human bones from stem cells in the laboratory, first for facial deformities, and then for much more.

VERY FIRST JOB: Babysitting. I had read the Baby-sitters Club. We had Excel spreadsheets for listing and doling out the jobs.

WHAT I WANTED TO BE WHEN I GREW UP: A reporter, a fashion designer (I sewed my own clothes), a judge. I had a lot of indecision about this. I loved theater and glee club.

A WEIRD THING YOU'D FIND ON (OR IN) MY DESK: My cat-shaped paper clips.

WORST SUBJECT IN SCHOOL: I got a bad grade in jewelry design. I was way too conceptual.

MY BEDTIME: If lucky, by ten-thirty p.m.

ON MY BUCKET LIST: I want to be a grandma.

A GUILTY PLEASURE: Mac and cheese. Long showers.

FAVORITE CANDY: Kettle corn popcorn.

FAVORITE CHILDHOOD BOOK: *A Wrinkle in Time.*

HOW OFTEN I CHECK MY BANK STATEMENT: We pay attention weekly. I know how much payroll is. I know how much rent is. That's what makes me a founder.

A TOOL I ALWAYS WANT TO HAVE IN MY HOUSE: My Leatherman or a tape measure.

ADVICE I'D GIVE TO MY THIRTEEN-YEAR-OLD SELF: Keep on being your weird self. Weird is great. Run with it. You're perfect.

Nina Tandon lives for science. She was married in a silk dress digitally printed with a wispy pink pattern made to resemble connective tissue in the body. Her now-husband gave her a 3-D-printed ring with a bone motif, featuring a lab-grown diamond (made out of carbon, just like real diamonds). She often wears a necklace that features a spiky EKG (which stands for electrocardiogram—it's like a line graph mapping the electrical activity of the heart). Yes, science finds its way into every aspect of her life.

It's no surprise, then, that Nina took aim at a biology feat that seems more science fiction than real world. Nina's bold goal in 2011: to be the first commercial business ever to grow human bones in a lab in three weeks flat. She called her start-up EpiBone (with the obvious Twitter handle @GrowYourOwnBone). One headline about EpiBone read, THIS COMPANY HAS PRETTY MUCH INVENTED HARRY POTTER'S "SKELE-GRO." Doesn't get much cooler.

After blood, bone is the most trans-planted human tissue. Every year, there are millions of procedures that involve cutting bone from one part of the body and using it to fix another. There are also countless synthetic implants being in-

Tip: Anytime you can be the first ever person or company to do something, the challenge is extreme but so is the payoff—financial and psychic—when you succeed.

serted, like fake knees and hips made from metal or plastic. Non-biological objects in the body can be rejected, and the fakes typically last around fifteen years. If you get injured at age fifteen or replace your left knee at sixty, these parts will almost certainly need replac-ing. Also, a piece of bone taken from the hip and inserted elsewhere often causes pain at the hip site. So there are lots of opportunities for improvement. Nina saw them all.

One headline about EpiBone read, THIS COMPANY HAS PRETTY MUCH INVENTED HARRY POTTER'S "SKELE-GRO."

Nina hit on her idea while working in a graduate school lab at Colum-bia University. A bioengineer, she was attempting to become a cell whisperer. That means she was working to learn the "language" nec-essary to coax a clump of heart cells (from a rat) to become a bit of tissue that actually beats. She made this happen. The tissue in her petri dish moved and went boom-boom, boom-boom.

Nina's fascination with human cells dates back to age ten. Her three siblings all had vision issues that were genetically based, making her curious to know more. Her sisters were color-blind, and her brother had night blindness. After having studied engineering in college, Nina started studying bioengineering. At one point, she worked on developing an electronic nose used to "smell" lung cancer.

By the time she reached Columbia, she was fully focused on human tissue and how to engineer its growth. She had a very smart lab mate named Sarindr Bhumiratana, who had a similar obsession; he was working with cells to get them to transform into bone. Now Sarindr is her cofounder, and they have pooled their learning and are growing small, custom bones starting from a few cells. The cells they use are called stem cells, which are the building blocks of all organs and cell types in the body. They act like generic cells that, in response to certain signals and chemicals, turn into basically any type of cell, whether a skin cell, a bone cell, or a blood cell.

Have you read the novel or seen the movie *Wonder*? The boy in the story was born with a facial bone deformity. That is exactly the type of issue Nina and her company, EpiBone, plan to fix. In fact, bones above the neck that are affected by cancer, dental surgery, trauma, or congenital anomalies are first up on EpiBone's agenda. "I get really excited about the idea of no kids with cranial or congenital disorders anymore," she said. She also expects to help a lot of wounded soldiers dealing with head injuries.

Here's how EpiBone's technology will work, if all goes according to plan: A customer—someone with a shattered bone due to trauma, for example—will come for a high-tech X-ray called a CT scan. The scan will provide a picture of the exact space that needs a replacement bone. From that picture, a 3-D program creates a model in the correct shape. Next, using a long (but not painful) needle, EpiBone scientists extract stem cells from abdominal fat. The cells are spread on a frame, placed in a bioreactor ("which is basically just like a fancy fish tank," Nina describes), and in three weeks, with the aid of nutrients and warmth from the tank, the cells will grow into the correct-shaped bone.

So far, the process has worked brilliantly with pig and rat cells, recreating pig jawbones and rat skulls. In 2020, Nina will start testing the process using human stem cells. She will apply for approval from the FDA before she can do this commercially. She has come so far but still must wait for so much to materialize.

Tip: Getting help is not a sign of weakness. It is a sign of strength. Find out who does know, and learn from them.

When Nina went to raise her first EpiBone funding in 2013, two years after starting up, she openly told investors they would have to be patient—the bone revolution would take time. "I said, 'If you're interested in WhatsApp, walk away. We're slow and steady, we're science nerds, and we are aiming to help humanity,'" she told *Inc.* magazine. In that first financing, she set out to raise $700,000 but walked away with $4 million! Now she's raised $13 million more, and counting.

She must be doing something right in meetings. But that side of the job—the wooing of investors, the business of business—didn't come naturally, even after earning an MBA following her bio-engineering PhD (yeah, that's lots of degrees!). To compensate for what she considers inexperience, she gets lots of coaching. "Start-ups are like the Olympics. If you're competing, you need a coach," she said. And it's not just her. All her employees work with coaches.

"I said, 'If you're interested in WhatsApp, walk away. We're slow and steady, we're science nerds, and we are aiming to help humanity.'"

To stay sane in such a busy job, Nina spends quiet mornings alone, doing yoga (which she's certified to teach), meditating, or running. Then she and her cofounder drive to their Brooklyn office together, and they catch up while commuting.

Many people ask Nina for advice on how to get girls to love STEM (science, technology, engineering, math). She says to turn them on to toys like GoldieBlox and littleBits. She also tells all girls who are good at math and science to double down on those subjects. "My dad always said, 'You should study the most technically difficult subject you can master, because that will give you a seat at the table.' Math and science are like French. Learn them young. It's much easier at age eight than later on," she says.

Her dad also taught her to always ask yourself when meeting someone new, *What can I offer them?* Her dad didn't realize it then, but he knew how to raise a CEO.

JESSICA O. MATTHEWS

FOUNDER AND CEO OF
UNCHARTED POWER

Business 101: You don't have to be a "techie" to invent something technologically revolutionary.

HER BUSINESS: Harnessing kinetic energy to produce green power for many uses. She started with soccer balls and now uses suitcase wheels, shopping carts, road bumps, and more!

A WEIRD THING YOU'D FIND ON (OR IN) MY DESK: A carved soccer ball made out of Moroccan wood.

WORST SUBJECT IN SCHOOL: Geography—Lord have mercy! I was under the impression that after the Civil War, Virginia and West Virginia got back together. They did not!

VERY FIRST JOB: I worked very briefly at the YWCA as a front-desk associate.

MY BEDTIME: When my body fails, against my will, I fall down.

ON MY BUCKET LIST: I want to be a hip-hop violinist.

A GUILTY PLEASURE: I really like *Million Dollar Listing* on Bravo.

AN EXPRESSION I USE A LOT THAT PEOPLE KNOW ME FOR: Inside the office I'll say, "This is a THING" (I mean this is worth our time).

FAVORITE CANDY: Pull 'n' Peel Twizzlers and Snickers.

FAVORITE CHILDHOOD BOOK: *The Great Doctors*. I got it around age eleven. Everything from Hippocrates to stealing cadavers. I read the heck out of it—the cover ripped, the whole thing ripped.

HOW OFTEN I CHECK MY SALES: As long as we have enough to get where we're going, I'm not focused on that.

A TOOL I ALWAYS WANT TO HAVE IN MY HOUSE: Superglue.

ADVICE I'D GIVE TO MY THIRTEEN-YEAR-OLD SELF: You are going to discover yourself from age ten to thirty. Make sure to wear extra padding.

In 2015, Jessica dressed as tennis star Serena Williams for Halloween. Some potential investors visited that day and she presented to them in costume. She did percussive step team in high school. She says "dope" a lot, while clicking along in her high pumps and black leggings. She studied psychology and economics at Harvard. She strives to be a cross of Beyoncé and Bill Nye the Science Guy; EVERYONE WANTS TO BE BEYONCÉ, BUT NOBODY WANTS TO PUT IN THE WORK is painted on her office wall. Jessica does the work.

She grew up in a town in eastern New York called Poughkeepsie (*Poo-KIP-see*). She says her Nigerian mom stressed achievement, as do many immigrant moms who have escaped an impoverished homeland and urgently want their kids to take full advantage of their privilege. Jessica remembers once watching an *Oprah Winfrey Show* episode about teen inventors with her sister. She was around the same age as the featured prodigies but hadn't earned a patent for some eye-popping innovation like the kids on-screen. "My mom asked us, 'What, are you *not allowed* to do what these kids are doing? Is that why you are just sitting here?'" Jessica recounts, laughing now but recalling feeling like an underachiever who should do better.

> **Tip:** Be very, very observant. Noticing things around you and picking up on trends is how the best ideas are born.

In less than a decade, Jessica would accomplish the very thing her mom was pressing for.

First, though, she would visit Nigeria for her aunt's wedding. It was 2006, and Jessica was seventeen. During the reception, the electricity went out. Blackouts are fairly common in parts of Nigeria, as are the stinky generators rolled out to provide a quick fix. Jessica tried not to hold her nose as the generators kicked out the equivalent of two packs of cigarettes. She feared for her Nigerian family's health! The fumes were still on her mind the following day when she noticed her nephew's soccer obsession—and so many boys like him. With a need for power sources on her brain, a thought bubble (just like in a cartoon) floated up above her head: *Kicking, energy, electricity . . . ?*

The thought bubble followed her all the way to college—Harvard—to her engineering for non-engineers class, where she'd been assigned a project to identify a problem and solve it using art and science. Jessica could easily identify a problem: the one billion or so people on our planet without regular electricity. And she definitely had a creative (maybe crazy) theory about how to fix it. . . .

She began **tinkering,** starting with a plastic hamster ball that was easy to take apart and reassemble and had space in its inner chamber for a shake-to-charge flashlight. It became her totally imperfect first stab at a chargeable ball. The supplies were nothing special, all from the drug-store. Mocking up an idea like this is called **prototyping.** Her advice for the initial phase of any invention: Don't get hung up on what the sell-able version is. Try things that are sort of like what you want, maybe similar in shape, or function, or materials, and just quick-assemble the parts with tape or even the elastic from ratty gym shorts. "You can in-novate a lot for a hundred dollars," she says.

Happy with her first take, she began kicking the prototype around. Tap. Tap. Tap. A quick dribbling session and the flashlight glowed. It worked!

After lots more rounds of experimenting and soldering (the most basic technique in circuit making, involving heated tools that melt wires to-gether, which are then attached to a circuit board, allowing electricity to flow), she had a working model. She likes telling girls that soldering circuits isn't any harder than giving yourself a gel manicure or a pin curl. You don't need to be a techie to figure it out—you just need to be curi-ous. When she was finished with her project, she'd created a pendulum inside a ball, which created friction, which produced enough electricity to charge a battery. Thirty minutes of dribbling produced six watts of output, or seventy-two hours of light. She then added an output plug in the ball's surface, where a lamp or phone could attach. That was it. Her playful little charger, later named Soccket, was born.

In 2011, she officially launched her company, Uncharted Play. To pro-duce her power balls in big quantities, she needed to raise money. She found a factory upstate and shipped them the parts. Her first $92,296 she raised on Kickstarter (from 1,094 donors), beating her goal of

$75,000. She was ecstatic when Bill Gates, Microsoft's founder, posted on social media about Soccket, and Ashton Kutcher, too. But despite attracting such famous fans, she struggled.

She strives to be a cross of Beyoncé and
Bill Nye the Science Guy.

Producing reliable Socckets turned out to be darn hard. Jessica had to apologize to all her Kickstarter funders twice, when balls were delayed at the manufacturer. Then the first ball model proved hinky, sometimes stopping its power charge after a few kicks (once when a reporter was writing a story on the wonder ball), sometimes deflating, sometimes never producing light at all.

Jessica kept working at it. And she never stopped looking for problems to solve. A visit to a Syrian refugee camp—where girls weren't allowed to play soccer—sparked Uncharted Play's next product. The refugee camp's culture was very conservative; there was a belief that girls running around created too much temptation for boys. Jumping rope, though, the girls could do inside. So Jessica followed the same playbook and made a power-generating rope she called Pulse.

By 2017, the kinks were worked out, and half a million Socckets and Pulses had been used in Africa and Latin America. President Obama had even juggled (and headed!) a Soccket as a catchy public relations (PR) stunt (see page 274) while visiting the Ubongo Power Plant in Tanzania, where he was announcing his new initiative to help bring more power to Africa. Previously, Jessica had been invited to the

White House to celebrate her notable invention in green energy, and he picked her ball to bring along on his trip as a prop to demonstrate the kind of creativity the United States could offer.

But Jessica didn't stop there. Her true breakthrough went way beyond the ball or the jump rope or any single product. It was the fundamental insight that motion could be harnessed as a power source, that any movable object—

Tip: Find your squad. People who totally get you. Then lean on them.

dog, bike, ball—could become a mini power plant. No one had tapped these everyday items for energy before. And this broadly applicable technique—Jessica calls it motion-based, off-grid, renewable energy, or MORE—has nearly limitless uses. Suddenly Jessica was being compared to Thomas Edison and Elon Musk, the guy who founded both Tesla and space travel company SpaceX, which meant he could send one of his fancy cars into space (he did this!). She really had become the Beyoncé of tech!

The $7 million she raised in 2016 is the largest venture capital investment received by a woman of color, ever.

Jessica admits she kind of freaks when she thinks about heading a giant power company, so she goes about work hour by hour, day by day. If she can win the day, she can win the week. If she can win the week, she can win the month. Her truest support network is a group of West African friends she found in New York. And every day, Jessica remembers to ask herself, *Am I happy?* She adjusts her life accordingly if the answer is no.

In 2017, she changed her company name from Uncharted Play, which made sense for the ball and jump rope, to Uncharted Power, signaling an expansion into all sorts of moving things that could be harnessed for electricity. Jessica and her team have now partnered to make bike wheels, strollers, speed bumps, moving walkways, floor panels, suitcases, dog collars, and much more into mini power factories. A bike-share program in Nigeria actu-

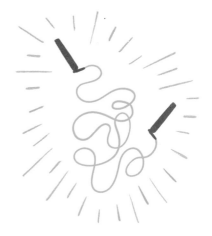

ally pays people to use bikes outfitted with Jessica's technology because they generate energy. She just filed a bunch of new patents, too. Like one for an "amalgamation circuit breakthrough that allows for the efficient combination of multiple microgenerators to be used in energy harvesting infrastructure development." (Beware—patents [see page 268] often contain lots of complicated legal jargon.)

Jessica is as concerned about empowering as she is about power. She knows it is rare to be black and female and working in tech, not to mention having founded a company. The $7 million she raised in 2016 is the largest venture capital investment received by a woman of color, ever. Even Disney has invested an undisclosed amount. She says she is "living a life of unlikelys." She wants to be a model for little girls who look like her, so to better achieve that end, she relocated Uncharted Power to Harlem, a majority African American neighborhood near the top of Manhattan. She has committed to supporting one hundred new start-ups in Harlem and training ten thousand residents in tech in five years. Talk about using her unique platform to transform a whole community and rev up the next generation of role models. Now, that is POWER-full!

JANE CHEN

COFOUNDER AND CEO OF
EMBRACE INNOVATIONS
AND **LITTLE LOTUS**

Business 101: Don't dismiss the cheap solution—
it can be the best solution.

HER BUSINESS: A nonelectric baby warmer called Embrace that has saved the lives of 300,000 premature babies in 22 developing countries. To fund her humanitarian work, she launched Little Lotus, selling temperature-regulating swaddling blankets for the US market in a "buy one, give one" model (made famous by TOMS shoes).

A WEIRD THING YOU'LL FIND ON (OR IN) MY DESK: A figurine of an angel holding a little boy. The mom of a boy an Embrace warmer saved gave it to me as a daily reminder of why I do my work.

VERY FIRST JOB: I collected spit at a viticulture (wine-making agriculture) lab at University of California, Davis.

AS A KID, WHAT I WANTED TO BE WHEN I GREW UP: A chef.

BEDTIME: Eleven p.m.

ON MY BUCKET LIST: Surfing in the Maldives.

A GUILTY PLEASURE: French fries and ice cream.

FAVORITE CANDY: Dark chocolate.

FAVORITE CHILDHOOD BOOK: *A Wrinkle in Time.*

ADVICE I'D GIVE TO MY THIRTEEN-YEAR-OLD SELF: If you can dream it and believe it, you can do it. I grew up doubting myself. I wish I hadn't.

Jane Chen's invention looks a lot like a miniature space suit or a sleeping bag sized for an American Girl doll. But don't let the simplicity of the design fool you. This is mad science at work, and with it Jane aims to save one million babies around the world.

Jane's journey to CEO began in graduate school at Stanford when she enrolled in a course called Designing for Extreme Affordability. The class mandate: Create solutions for people living on less than one dollar per day. Jane and her team chose to work on baby incubators. Her professor told her she would have to build one for less than 1 percent of the cost of the state-of-the-art model, so for $200 rather than $20,000.

Imagine cupping an apple in your palms—that's about the size of a preemie baby. Now consider that every year, 15 million babies are born prematurely—without enough body fat or organ development to stay alive without an outside source of heat. In developed countries, incubators keep those preemies alive. In remote villages, where resources are scarce, about 4 million preemie babies die every year.

This was a chance to save lives on a massive scale.

While developing the incubator concept in 2007, Jane had the opportunity to fly to Nepal to observe and interview future "customers." These were doctors, nurses, mothers, and midwives in villages in Asia and Africa.

In the medical clinics she visited, many things stood out. Very obvious: Many of the infants were not wearing diapers! Diapers were too expensive for most families. So any fabrics used in the warmer had to be easy to wipe down. Also, some of the clinics had a great modern incubator sitting around unused. Donated by well-intentioned charities, these modern devices either didn't work—broken parts that could not be fixed—or relied on electricity that wasn't readily available. Jane's warmer would have to heat without electricity and be made of a few uncomplicated parts. And it would have to be easily accessible, with a clear viewing window so doctors could monitor a baby's coloring—an important indicator of health.

> **Tip:** Wherever possible, observe your customers in their natural habitat—going about their daily lives on their own turf—as you seek to make products that very specifically meet their needs. Nothing substitutes for seeing your target user yourself, in action. Take careful notes.

This was a chance to save lives on a massive scale.

But there was more. Many women delivered at home and found it too taxing to travel the distance to a care facility afterward. The warmer would have to come to them. The invention had to be portable and easy for a nonmedical person to use.

And finally, the new incubator (like all incubators) needed to maintain a constant temperature, to keep the baby's body temp steady round the clock.

So at home in California, how did Jane, a business major, and her codevelopers, three engineering students, solve for *all* that? "We went back to high school chemistry and physics," Jane says. They knew that a substance undergoing a change of state (liquid to solid, for instance) maintains a constant temperature. If they could find a material that shifted states at exactly human body temperature—98 degrees—and did so very, very slowly, they could harness it to create steady heat for their baby warmer. They found their miracle waxlike material—one that changed from liquid to solid at precisely 98 degrees—by, oh, "just googling," says Jane with a laugh.

Next, they created a little pouch in their baby warmer to hold a sealed sandwich bag containing their magic material. The bag is meant to travel back and forth, from sink to the pouch, every eight hours or so. At the sink, it's run under hot water until the substance inside melts, becoming soft and flexible. (When they made their first model, they used butter in a ziplock bag to simulate the concept. Mega-messy!) Then it's returned to the incubator, where it will remain soft and warm for approximately eight hours. When the material becomes hard again, it's removed from the pouch and run under hot water again. In other words, the only maintenance required by anyone—doctor, mom, midwife—is a quick inspection of the bag to see if it's soft or hard.

Jane named the warmer Embrace. She knew she had a breakthrough invention when she started showing it around out of school: she (and team) won an innovation contest and received a funding grant. The message from these wins was clear: this invention was far too useful to pack away in a closet, just a memento of a cool class project. It had to be out in the world, saving babies.

Jane decided to create a company to bring Embrace to market, and to locate the headquarters in India, close to the manufacturers she'd chosen and close to Embrace's main customers (India is home to 40 percent of the world's premature and underweight babies). By 2010, the incubator was rolling out of factories and into homes and clinics.

Jane's chosen path of running a risky start-up in India did not go over well with her parents. They'd brought her from Taiwan to the United States when she was four. Like many new immigrants, their priority was getting their children into stable, high-paying careers. Jane's dad insisted that she become a doctor. "As a kid, he didn't let me introduce myself as Jane. I had to say 'Dr. Chen,'" she says, laughing. They came to accept her decision to attend business school instead of med school. But afterward, when Jane followed her heart and her business to India, they were upset that she wasn't pursuing a more practical career. What made her parents eventually embrace Embrace? "Me getting invited to the White House and getting a picture with Obama!" she says. She was asked there to participate in an innovation summit.

Embrace Innovations was formed initially as a nonprofit organization, raising all funding from grants and giving the warmers away in impoverished countries. But in 2011, with the product showing good results, Jane believed she could evolve the concept into more of a mixed for-profit/nonprofit model. The savvy CEO noticed that there were plenty of customers—government agencies and outfits like the World Health Organization, for instance—who would be willing to pay for incubators. So she began to charge the customers who could pay, and the money from sales went straight back into the nonprofit to fund donations. It was a great combination because it freed the nonprofit from the need for constant fund-raising.

But Jane wasn't done innovating. In 2014, after observing that all babies—chubby, underweight, healthy, sick—slept better in her Embrace warmers, Chen struck on a new business idea, one that would do even more to achieve her nonprofit's goals. She launched a sister company called Little Lotus. This new company also focused on body-temp-regulation items for babies—swaddles and blankets—but mostly in the United States.

When Jane followed her heart and her business to India, her parents were upset that she wasn't pursuing a more practical career. What made them eventually embrace Embrace? "Me getting invited to the White House and getting a picture with Obama!"

Little Lotus products feature technology inspired by NASA space suits. For example, tiny droplets of a waxlike substance on the fabric's surface modulate temperature by drawing away excess heat when babies get too warm and releasing it when they start to cool down.

Then, in 2014, Beyoncé entered the picture. The singer had had premature babies and was sensitive to and deeply moved by Jane's work. At a charity event featuring Jane's products, Beyoncé made a special appearance—in a white jumpsuit, no less—and the cameras didn't stop clicking, bringing great attention to Jane's cause. "She told me how incredible she thought the innovation was. I think what struck me was how sweet and genuine she was," Jane told a reporter at the time. "One of my most memorable moments of the night was getting to dance with her after we spoke," she added. And after the utterly magical night, Beyoncé sent her $125,000 to fund distribution of Embrace warmers in ten sub-Saharan African countries.

But don't let one big number fool you. Money was tight. And after five years as CEO, Jane found out how close to the edge she was playing. For a year, she had been deep in talks with a major medical device company that wanted to distribute the warmers, in exchange for cash to help sustain her business. This was a dream solution to many challenges Jane and her team faced. But just days from the deal closing, Jane picked up her *Wall Street Journal* and saw that the CEO at this major company, the guy who was championing the partnership, had been fired. Instantly, the deal was off.

At this moment, Embrace had sixty employees and less than seven days' worth of operating funds. Jane needed money FAST or they were going to have to close. "I couldn't bear the thought of losing it all. Day three or four of the crisis, I'm not sleeping. I'm freaking out. I'm racking my brain thinking about what we could possibly do," she says.

Who can save us? Who can save us? she thought over and over. "I'm calling everybody I know," she says, but no one stepped up to help. Then she had her best idea *ever.*

Nine months earlier, she had shown up for a predawn meditation session while attending a big economics conference in Switzerland attended by lots of politicians, leaders, and CEOs. She plopped down next to a man who introduced himself as Marc Benioff. They started chatting, and it turned out that they were both intent on saving premature babies. He had just given a big donation to a major initiative working on solutions. The pair quickly bonded, and traded emails. Benioff is one of America's richest men; he is CEO of a giant software company called Salesforce.

Now, on the brink of disaster, she emailed Benioff, explaining her dire situation. He wrote back within a day. He would happily provide the funding she needed.

Tip: Nobody will fault you for raising the red flag and calling "HELP!" when things are desperate. Getting bailed out starts with asking for help.

With the wind from this miracle at her back, Jane did something for herself she had been putting off for a decade: she learned to surf. She had delayed and dodged getting in the water due to fear. Fear of big waves. Fear of being out of control. Fear of getting squashed by her board. Fear of failure. Suddenly, with Benioff's generosity giving her great faith in all that is possible, she was ready to face down her terror. A few lessons in Hawaii launched an obsession with hanging ten that continues to grow today. She writes all about her adventures on her board in her blog, *Hanging Zen.*

What does Jane's surfing have to do with business? It has taught her some of life's most fundamental lessons, like the importance of waiting, being ready to ride whatever your day throws at you, how to be present, and to wade in without always having an end goal. "Each time I go into the ocean, I have to 'surrender to the power and beauty of nature. For someone who's not used to 'surrendering,' it's a novel feeling—a method of learning that is completely new, humbling, and mind-blowing all at the same time," she writes.

While surfing is deeply centering for Jane, so are the stories of kids and families in developing countries whose lives have been changed forever by her warmer. There is one story Jane has told hundreds of times and will tell hundreds more. A few years ago in China, a baby named Nathan was abandoned on the side of the road and brought to an orphanage. He weighed two pounds. Luckily, the orphanage had been given an Embrace warmer. For thirty days, he stayed inside the puffy light blue pouch, maintaining a steady body temperature. The facility had never seen a baby that small survive. But Nathan did! He was later adopted by a family in Chicago, where he was thriving and joyful, and his new mother reached out to personally thank Jane. She was overcome with emotion hearing this true affirmation of her mission. For his birthday, she sent him his own Embrace warmer, as a keepsake.

Talk about a warm embrace all around.

JEWELRY/ ACCESSORIES

EMILY NÚÑEZ CAVNESS

COFOUNDER AND CEO OF
SWORD & PLOUGH

Business 101: Doing good while doing well is
the ultimate win.

HER BUSINESS: Bags and jewelry made from recycled military gear, with a dual mission of employing veterans.

VERY FIRST JOB: A newspaper route in sixth grade, which I did every morning for an entire year with my brother and sister.

AS A KID, WHAT I WANTED TO BE WHEN I GREW UP: An astronaut (like my uncle).

A WEIRD THING YOU'D FIND ON (OR IN) MY DESK: Awesome Sword & Plough glass coasters that my mom fused and made herself.

WORST SUBJECT IN SCHOOL: Physics.

MY BEDTIME: Eleven p.m.

ON MY BUCKET LIST: Get a degree from Stanford business school (which she is doing).

A GUILTY PLEASURE: Vanilla ice cream.

AN EXPRESSION I USE A LOT THAT PEOPLE KNOW ME FOR: "Guess what!"

FAVORITE CANDY: Chocolate.

FAVORITE CHILDHOOD BOOK: *Too Many Pumpkins.*

HOW OFTEN I CHECK MY SALES: Daily.

ADVICE I'D GIVE TO MY THIRTEEN-YEAR-OLD SELF: Step out of your comfort zone often.

SOMETHING YOU'LL ALWAYS FIND IN MY FRIDGE: Raspberries and cheese.

Picture yourself inside a military tent in Afghanistan filled with tired workout equipment left over from the 1980s. Outside it's a toasty 108 degrees Fahrenheit, which means inside it's also a roasty 108 (no air-conditioning on a dusty military post in the Kandahar province). You're twenty-four years old, the only gal in the room, which means you demonstrated considerable skill to get here, but you're also a little lonely. While the guys grunt over barbells together and admire their glistening pecs, you pump iron alone. At least you brought earbuds and a smartphone. Piping into your ears: the audiobook of *Lean In,* Facebook exec Sheryl Sandberg's manifesto urging women to go for it in business. It's getting to you, in a good way.

That was Emily Núñez Cavness's experience while on deployment in 2013. She was an assistant intelligence officer in the 4th Engineer Battalion of the US Army, and her job was figuring out where the Taliban had planted roadside bombs. She was operating entirely in a man's world, and Sheryl Sandberg was telling her—literally whispering into her ears—how to make it work. "I stopped backing away from sitting at the table for the commander's update brief. I focused on sounding more decisive. And when I received praise, I practiced saying 'thank you' instead of fighting it," Emily says.

Tip: Receiving praise graciously is a huge sign of confidence. Don't blush and refuse a compliment. Accept the kind words unapologetically. Next step: Boast occasionally, when you deserve to. #shebrag

It was all good practice for war and for business. Unbeknownst to many of her fellow officers, Emily had a foot in both worlds. Before being shipped out to the remote desert, Emily and her sister Betsy had founded a company called Sword & Plough. Their idea was to turn used military gear into stylish, sturdy bags.

The Sword & Plough idea had come to Emily a few months before deployment. She'd been sitting in the Middlebury College campus lunchroom. The school was popular with environmentalist students, and being around them heightened Emily's consciousness about waste. She had lived a life surrounded by military gear: Her dad was a logistician in the army. Her uncle was a test pilot in the Marine Corps and worked NASA missions as an astronaut. She and Betsy had spent their childhoods moving to various military bases. What happened to all those boxes of tents and parachutes and uniforms deemed past their time? They were stored away in musty attics or burned in stinky fires or thrown into landfills. Could she give all that gear a second life?

She loved the idea that the gear that outfitted such patriotic people would have a respectful retirement. She could turn it into durable, practical, military-chic bags. She would hire as many veterans as possible.

Within weeks, she was pitching her bags at a business plan competition on Middlebury's campus. "I was so nervous," she says. "I had no experience with developing a business plan. My husband [then boyfriend] encouraged me to tell my personal story. Why I was so passionate about the idea." It worked. People liked her concept at Middlebury—she won first prize ($3,000) *and* at Harvard, where she pitched her plan later that winter, during a blizzard. (Imagine Emily and Betsy in heels and dresses, begging a ride on a snowplow to make it there on time. They really did this.)

Tip: When pitching your idea, DO make it personal. Why do you want this business? What happened in your life that got you to this idea? Real emotions hook people.

Everything was going great. Then Emily learned just weeks after graduation that her deployment time had come. It was 2013, and she was headed to Afghanistan. A professor friend helped her petition to delay a few months in order to attend a start-up mentoring program sponsored by Dell called Social Innovation Lab. There, an advisor suggested the name Sword & Plough. This was a reference from the Bible, "to turn swords into ploughshares," which means making something good from something bad. That was it!

After completing her seven-month tour in Afghanistan, she and Betsy launched a Kickstarter project with a goal of raising $20,000. They spread the word on Facebook, starting with friends and family. They also cold-called news editors and scored coverage in *Bloomberg Inc.* and *Entrepreneur.* They beat their fund-raising target tenfold! That was good. But now they owed each of their 1,500 backers a thank-you bag made from recycled military gear. They'd have to produce those—fast!

They did. And to date, they have recycled over thirty thousand pounds of military surplus. Their High Impact Tote Bag (costing $99), army-green top and camo bottom, is a Sword & Plough bestseller. They have provided sixty-five jobs to veterans and have five veteran-owned manufacturers making bags. The whole adventure has been very star-studded for Emily. She has appeared on *Good Morning America, Fox & Friends,* and *The Today Show.* She has gotten to meet President Obama at the White House, Gayle King at the Forbes Women's Summit, and Sheryl Sandberg at the Pentagon. Yes, cue the military band!

Emily learned just weeks after graduation that her deployment time had come. It was 2013, and she was headed to Afghanistan.

But Emily is truly split in her allegiances—half of herself in the business, the other half on the battlefield. So in 2015, when the US Army announced that women would be allowed to train to become Army Rangers for the first time, Emily raised her hand. The most top secret, dangerous, and physically demanding army jobs are performed by Rangers. "It was too good a development not to try," Emily says. "I wanted to show the army that this was something women were excited about. To try even if I failed." She had to perform seven pull-ups. At the start she could only do one. Of course, she mastered the pull-ups. She gained fifteen pounds of muscle while training. Her hair, then to her elbows, had to be hacked off. No longer than one inch! In the end, she didn't gain entry to the Rangers. But she is terribly proud to have tried and come close.

To date, they have recycled over thirty thousand pounds of military surplus.

She brings the soldier and the business halves of herself to work every day, finding new ways to bridge the divide, like her company's cool new uniform recycling program. The company provides a free mailing label, and families around the country can mail in uniforms of any age. One man sent in cavalry pants he wore in World War I. Oftentimes clothes arrive with letters full of memories and photos. A veteran in Colorado then cuts the vintage uniforms into small squares, which become pockets on new bags. Also new: Sword & Plough jewelry. A veteran Emily and Betsy learned about makes necklaces, earrings, and stackable rings by hand-hammering used .50-caliber bullet casings. They contract with her now.

Most businesses operate around a "bottom line," business lingo for the annual amount of money that must come in to keep a business afloat while maximizing profits. Emily and Betsy have constructed a "quadruple bottom line"—a blend of for-profit ideas and for-the-good-of-humanity ideals that lets them sleep at night. The quad includes making a profit, giving work to veterans, helping the environment by recycling, and giving old fabrics a new life, out of respect. Yes, a quadruple win.

HANNAH LAVON

COFOUNDER AND CEO OF **HOORAY HOOPLA**
AND CREATOR OF **PALS**

Business 101: Seasonal businesses are especially tricky. Find a product that people need year-round.

HER BUSINESS: Mismatched socks meant to inspire kids to dare to be different.

A WEIRD THING YOU'LL FIND ON (OR IN) MY DESK: Lots of robotic bugs like cockroaches. My cat, Sweet Potato, is very needy, and this way she can bat them around and I can concentrate.

HIGH SCHOOL GPA: I had a B-plus and I'm fine with it. I went to art school and the school was fine with it.

WORST SUBJECT IN SCHOOL: Math. I had all kinds of tutors. I had a learning disability and got double time on tests. It's super ironic because now my job is basically all math.

VERY FIRST JOB: I taught myself Photoshop and made sign boards and posters and CD covers for kids' bar and bat mitzvahs.

AS A KID, WHAT I WANTED TO BE WHEN I GREW UP: An astronaut. I still kind of want to be one.

MY BEDTIME: Twelve-thirty a.m.

ON MY BUCKET LIST: Go to outer space.

A GUILTY PLEASURE: Cinnamon buns.

FAVORITE CANDY: Fun Dip. Also rock candy—I love pure sugar.

FAVORITE CHILDHOOD BOOK: *The Stinky Cheese Man.*

HOW OFTEN I CHECK MY BANK STATEMENT: Twice a month. I have a bookkeeper. I check when I need to pay bills.

A TOOL I ALWAYS WANT TO HAVE IN MY HOUSE: A plunger. You never know when you are going to need it.

SOME WORDS TO LIVE BY: If you don't try, you'll never know. Life motto for sure.

Hannah describes her Long Island, New York, middle school as "a very fit-in-or-die situation." This was the 1990s, and girls were walking around with Prada and Kate Spade bags, wearing Dolce & Gabbana. Her mom, on the other hand, was a feminist who wanted nothing to do with fancy status-symbol brands. She gave Hannah her own copy of *Our Bodies, Ourselves,* which is a big book about periods, boobs, and all kinds of personal women's stuff. (Ask your mom about it. Good chance she has a copy.) So from an early age, Hannah didn't fit in. She had a stutter and lacked confidence. But her mom always believed in her and boosted her up—Hannah credits her mom with helping her come to accept herself.

She was always artsy, into cartoons and photography. She went to art school at Syracuse University, and when she finished she worked in advertising as an art director. Way back then, she had a goal to be her own boss by age thirty. Working at night, she partnered with a co-worker, Ashley, and they invested $600 and started a quirky little business they called Hooray Hoopla. They first made mugs with slogans and cards with funny sayings; they called their line My Punny Valentines. They then wanted to produce and sell something more substantial, and Hannah identified a product that she'd always wanted for herself. It started as a zany doodle in her sketchbook: mittens that were opposing characters (like cat and mouse), the sort that could have silly hand fights on the subway or in the grocery line. There was wolf vs. sheep and frog vs. fly. They called the mitten brand Vs (as in *versus*).

> **Tip:** Set goals for yourself, both big, far-off ones and small, doable-right-now ones. Having a goal out there on the horizon helps direct your path now. Goals are a way of translating dreams into specific, actionable steps.

To get past the idea phase, they found a woman on Craigslist who crocheted and hired her to make a sample. Then they found a website that listed factories, and they located one that would be willing to make the mittens. The mittens sold well in the winter holiday season, but come February, all the stores had them on markdown. In spring and summer—forget it. They needed a concept that would appeal year-round. A concept like . . . mismatched socks.

It was the same mismatch concept as the mittens—but reversed. Instead of being enemies, the sock pairs were friends. This new product line they called Pals. Dragons and unicorns? Friends! Even wolf and sheep friends! "Sending out good vibes is one of the most important things you can do," Hannah says. In fact, sending out good vibes is why she pursued the sock project. Without a higher purpose, she'd just be putting more *stuff* into the world. One of the marketing slogans Hannah adopted for the socks is "De*feet* the norm." In other words: just because dragons and unicorns might not normally hang doesn't mean they can't. Same with T. rexes and triceratops (that combo, by the way, is Pals's bestseller).

It started as a zany doodle in her sketchbook.

The first store that sold the sock pairs was UncommonGoods, an online retailer of oddball stuff like build-your-own-robot kits and avocado tree starter kits. But once the order came in, the Pals duo had to figure out how to come up with the money to get the socks produced. Factories, all the good ones in Asia (because Asian factories are the only ones they could find that could execute the complicated designs), insisted on sewing a minimum of three thousand pairs per style. And they'd only accept cash. Up front. Pals took out a $25,000 small business loan, and it was just enough to keep them afloat. Now, three years later, Pals is in more of a power position. They can be choosier about which factories they hire to do their manufacturing. Asian factories have been known to abuse human rights, so Pals seeks out those rated to have the best conditions.

Creating the sock designs, developing creative marketing ideas, and dreaming up new products are Hannah's favorite parts of her job.

Hannah creates the designs in a program called Adobe Illustrator and uploads the files to the factory. After a few weeks, samples arrive in the mail. She gives feedback and then gets another round of samples.

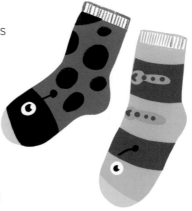

Hannah's least favorite part of the job is asking people to pay overdue bills. "You want them to keep doing business with you, but you also need to be forceful. I'm not a good forceful person," she admits.

Hannah admits that **cash flow** is an ongoing struggle. Even now, selling socks in four hundred stores, and bringing in about $25,000 weekly in strong weeks and $5,000 weekly in the summertime (when socks sound dreadful), Hannah consistently has to borrow from friends and family to manage cash flow. She quickly pays them back. This is not just Pals's struggle but the struggle of small businesses everywhere, because there is almost never a big stash in the bank to bridge the time between paying for production and receiving the money from sales.

> **Tip:** Understand what your customers like and want rather than just going with what you like and want.

She thinks it's funny that so much of her job is math, considering she went into art and thought she'd never need math again. "The bottom line of a business is a lot of it is math," she says. "Creating a cool concept is like one percent of the job." Her cofounder, Ashley, had been handling more of the operations side of the business, but in 2018 she left the company fully. The partnership was no longer working well, in part because Ashley never felt ready to quit her full-time job; she was always torn between risky sock start-up and stable ad agency. Hannah's takeaway is that it pays to be very clear about expectations like commitment level up front. She and Ashley were not.

Hannah's absolute favorite sock design ever is bird and worm—worm is brown. Apparently brown socks are just a NO, so they didn't sell. A big lesson for Hannah has been that she and her customers aren't always on the same wavelength. And that's OKAY.

"Sending out good vibes is one of the most important things you can do," Hannah says. In fact, sending out good vibes is why she pursued the sock project. Without a higher purpose, she'd just be putting more stuff into the world.

She constantly has new ideas. Right now she's thinking about creating clear rain boots, so the socks show through underneath. She might do pj's, slippers, and her mismatched mittens again. "But this time around I'll make the two mittens friends instead of enemies," she says.

MAKEUP

LESLIE BLODGETT

EXECUTIVE CHAIRPERSON OF
BARE ESCENTUALS
AND CREATOR OF
BAREMINERALS

Business 101: Make your customers feel like friends.

HER BUSINESS: A massive worldwide makeup brand centered on their most celebrated innovation—mineral-based cosmetics.

VERY FIRST JOB: McDonald's.

AS A KID, WHAT I WANTED TO BE WHEN I GREW UP: Actress.

A WEIRD THING YOU'LL FIND ON (OR IN) MY DESK: I have letters from my son when he was ten, which I still look at.

WORST SUBJECT IN SCHOOL: Social studies.

MY BEDTIME: Nine p.m.

ON MY BUCKET LIST: Well, I already met Oprah. I went to a luncheon at her house and sat two seats away. She kissed me! So, bucket list— I want to be in a movie.

A GUILTY PLEASURE: Potato chips.

AN EXPRESSION I USE A LOT THAT PEOPLE KNOW ME FOR: "You've gotta freakin' be kidding me." "Oh my god, that's awesome!"
FAVORITE CANDY: Peppermint Patties.
A TOOL I ALWAYS WANT TO HAVE IN MY HOUSE: A blow-dryer.
ADVICE I'D GIVE TO MY THIRTEEN-YEAR-OLD SELF: Make anxiety your friend instead of trying to push it away.

Leslie has opened Bare Escentuals all-company staff meetings by jumping onstage and right into the splits. She once led a group dance to a Rihanna song. When she needed retail distribution and makeup giant Sephora would not give her the time of day, she rented a white limo, picked up several Sephora execs (their offices were just down the street), and invited them for makeovers. Pretty out-there, as executives go.

The *New York Times* called Leslie the most significant female influencer in the beauty industry since Estée Lauder. She freaked when she read the headline to that article (*Move Over, Estée Lauder*). She was idolized for growing Bare Escentuals from a rinky-dink, failing aromatherapy bath and body chain into a cosmetics powerhouse that Shiseido paid $1.7 billion for in 2016.

> *She always refused media training and a professional script, believing that the minute her words sounded fake and salesy, women would stop listening.*

Leslie's makeup reign began with a massive gamble on August 31, 1997. Her offbeat plan was to go on QVC, a television home-shopping network that hosts nonstop infomercials, to tell the world about the mineral-based line she was launching. No one in the cosmetics industry had ever tried to sell on this twenty-four-hour TV network. People told her she was nuts. But she was desperate to help people understand this new form of chemical-free, loose-powder face makeup that she was betting her company on. She knew pasty pancake makeup and liquid foundation, which everyone was wearing, was yuck and would give way to the light, natural coverage of minerals *if only she could show women the way.* The makeup application required some technique and a long explanation. She didn't invent mineral makeup; the company had already developed one or two mineral items when she arrived as the new CEO. But she made it *a thing. A mega thing,* in fact.

Turned out, she was a complete TV pro. She put on a simple but pleasing white suit and she talked to the camera like she was gabbing with her best girlfriend, teaching her some "awesome" makeup tips (Leslie says "awesome" constantly). Looking straight into the camera, she said, "Do you want to make your skin break out with zits even more? Then don't try my product. But if you're interested in something pure that you can actually sleep in, then let's talk." She always refused media training and a professional script, believing that the minute her words sounded fake and salesy, women would stop listening. "What made it unique is I was an average person, not a model, not an actress. I'm a regular person who looks like a regular person."

Leslie's first QVC appearance wiped out her mineral makeup supply. She sold $45,000 worth. During her second QVC go, she sold $180,000 of foundation in ten minutes. Soon she was selling $1.4 million in makeup an hour.

The money was great. And she knew she was the newly anointed queen of makeup when over one hundred copycats sprang up. Every single makeup brand was introducing their own mineral makeup. It got irritating to have so many people sending links, asking, "Have you seen this?" The copycats didn't matter. Her mineral foundation became the number-one-selling brand. Her company came out with every form of mineral makeup possible. There was blush, eye shadow, bronzer, even a bagel schmear (no, kidding on that one).

Being close to her customers has always been Leslie's secret tactic. She talked to them directly through infomercials. She wrote back to their questions and comments in the QVC online portal. She visited malls and had big crowds vote on their favorite products. She plastered her twenty-third-floor San Francisco office with love letters from fangirls around the world, people who wrote to say that before Leslie's makeup they had never felt beautiful. She wrote back to plenty of those admirers, by hand. She hugs the women who line up outside her store openings. She has even made house calls to meet and do makeup with women who swear by bareMinerals. That constant, direct feedback, she believes, is what has made her products so great. Her team basically cocreated the new makeup with customers.

Tip: Forge a personal connection with your customers. Get out there and hang out with them. If you truly bond like sisters, you will definitely sell more.

But behind the scenes there are other reasons for Leslie's success. Leslie believes picking the right spouse or life partner is one of the biggest decisions impacting an entrepreneur's success. (Facebook second-in-command Sheryl Sandberg says the same thing in *Lean In*.) Leslie's husband stayed home, and she was the breadwinner. "The bareMinerals story is as much about him as it is about me," she often says. He loved cooking and caring for their son. Every day at three p.m. he called the office to see what Leslie wanted for dinner. Because he wasn't jealous or resentful, she felt that she could work as hard as and travel as much as she needed to.

> **Tip:** Marriage or partnering up romantically is a superlong way off, yes, but tuck this thought away. Pick a supportive, hands-on, not-afraid-to-change-poopy-diapers, and most important, a proud-to-see-you-run-the-world mate.

Looking at her now, it seems like Leslie just glided to the top, and everything happened with ease. That is so not true. She speaks with a bit of a lisp and has been mocked for it on Twitter (and her whole life). She dropped out of the State University of New York, where she went to study modern dance after high school. She moved to Florida and was waitressing at Ponderosa Steakhouse when her mom, who panicked her daughter would never launch in life, made her apply to the Fashion Institute of Technology. Leslie has a sister who she barely spoke to for about a decade.

Early attempts to get makeup industry jobs were all fails, and she certainly paid her dues, doing low-level jobs once she did manage to break in. Getting hired at the Bloomingdale's makeup counter required her pestering the employment staff nonstop. She literally camped out outside their office. From there, she worked the Ultima II counter at Macy's, on one occasion modeling eight shades of eye shadow at once. She later interned at Revlon and did product development on colorless mascara at Max Factor. Then Neutrogena hired her. All this experience is what led the flailing Bare Escentuals head, in 1995, to woo her as CEO. It wasn't some prize gig. He was an old friend. The business was bombing. It was a serious gamble for her. She was the family moneymaker; they had a kid. This was RISKY.

> **Tip:** Girls are often afraid to be seen as pesky, but sometimes aggressiveness is necessary. Pick your battles so you get results but not a bad reputation.

When she sold the company to Shiseido in 2016, she didn't leave, as is customary. She really couldn't—for customers, she *was* the brand. Only two years later, in 2018, did she finally cut the cord. She was truly itching for new creative pursuits and fresh challenges.

Soon she was selling $1.4 million in makeup an hour.

Leslie wants a second big act. She hasn't figured out what that is yet, but she is busy exploring. She has gone back to college at Stanford University, in a program encouraging multigenerational mixing by inviting older folks to attend classes alongside traditional younger students. (She dresses in her skullcap, hiking boots, and backpack, hoping to fit in. "My whole life has been about fitting in. That's why women trusted me," she says.) Right now, she's studying acting and writing there. She is also working on a book. She just became a grandma and does lots of babysitting (and posting of brag shots of her grandson on social media). She helps female entrepreneurs and funds some of their ventures, including Tina Sharkey's Brandless (page 235). She is on Sara Blakely's advisory board at Spanx (page 11), and on the board of directors at Every Mother Counts, a nonprofit founded by model Christy Turlington Burns to help prevent deaths in pregnancy and childbirth.

When you're this invested in business and leading, you never truly leave it behind; you just figure out where to plug yourself in next. Stay tuned for Leslie's next move.

KATIA BEAUCHAMP

COFOUNDER AND CEO OF
BIRCHBOX

Business 101: Big problem = Big opportunity.

HER BUSINESS: A subscription-box service bringing fun cosmetic samples to customers' doors regularly so they can try out products before committing to an expensive purchase.

A WEIRD THING YOU'LL FIND ON (OR IN) MY DESK: Bright pink Air Force 1 Nikes.

AN EXPRESSION I USE A LOT THAT PEOPLE KNOW ME FOR: "We don't hear no."

SOMETHING THAT DRIVES ME CRAZY: People standing in their own way—who don't understand they can drive [their own life].

LEAST FAVORITE PART OF MY JOB: Anything involving politics or bureaucracy, when you need to be censored.

ALWAYS IN MY FRIDGE: Sriracha.

A GUILTY PLEASURE: Dumplings.

WORST HABIT: Being extremely demanding.

SOMETHING I WISH I HAD INVENTED: The light bulb.

Katia can lay claim to having launched the trendiest of modern phenomena: the subscription box. Sure, there'd been book of the month clubs and shoe of the month clubs, and produce crates from nearby farms, but there was nothing like what we've got today. Clothes in a box (Stitch Fix—page 27), candles in a box (Vellabox), baking ingredients in a box (Whisk & Flour), soccer in a box (The Soccer Society), dog and cat stuff in a box (BarkBox and KitNipBox). And on and on.

Katia and her cofounder and co-CEO (and before that close friend), Hayley, broke the field wide-open with cosmetics in a box. They targeted the seven-billion-dollar industry early, recognizing it as a rare category: it's ginormous, and the unlimited options the internet serves up make shopping *harder.* The box model solves the problem of too many options and too little information. Who would drop sixty-two dollars on a body serum they haven't rubbed on? Birchbox hit their five-year sales target in the first seven months of operation.

Indeed, Katia rocketed from denim-clad El Paso high schooler in the late nineties to Harvard Business School student in 2008 to Birchbox cofounder and CEO to the cover of *Fortune* magazine in 2013. For a time, Birchbox was valued at half a billion dollars.

From the start, Katia's superstrength was the **cold email.** (Remember the cold call, where you have to be persuasive enough to sell to a stranger in five minutes flat? This is similar, but you do it with your fingers.) In 2010, while still a student at Harvard, Katia had to convince a bunch of trendy beauty brands to give her hundreds of samples and to let her sell them in adorable boxes on Birchbox.com. She had nothing to offer them but her business plan and a lot of big talk. She told them she aimed to fix the beauty industry's central problem: Customers want to try before they buy. She sure must have been convincing. . . .

What was the science (and art) to her killer cold-emailing? (Grab your highlighter—here comes some serious know-how.) The subject line must be enticing and not sound like spam. Her go-to subject line: *reimagining beauty on the internet*. The email must be *very* brief. She always tests her note on her phone to ensure that no scrolling is required (no scrolling—make it your mantra). She makes a very specific request, one small enough that you'd have to be a jerk to say no. For instance, *Can I have five minutes of your time to ask one or two questions?* A fun aside: She once cold-emailed Steve Jobs directly, guessing his email address, annoyed that everyone on the Harvard campus was buying IBM computers and Apple wasn't offering any student deals on her beloved Macs. Someone from Steve's team wrote right back saying Mr. Jobs would like to extend her a special discount.

Maybe Katia was so savvy at wooing strangers because as a "too skinny," "definitely not fashionable" girl in Texas, she switched middle schools and was forced to learn how to adjust on the fly. She broke into existing friendship groups and convinced them to make room for her; she got accepted to the cheerleading squad with little experience, at a time when all the other girls had been groomed for high kicking since birth.

Katia has rare confidence. She always had "irrational certainty" that Birchbox could work. She views success as a self-fulfilling prophecy, meaning that things you believe to be, come to be. Believing is what makes them happen. "I really believe that you can create reality," she said.

> **Tip:** Stay in touch with people who help you. Drop them a note periodically. These are your champions, and you will need them again. Plus, you have lots to learn from them.

The first brand to respond affirmatively to one of Katia's cold emails, agreeing to a quick call, then an in-person meeting in California, and finally to becoming Birchbox's first partner-brand, was Benefit Cosmetics. Katia still keeps in touch with Benefit's global CEO, who gave her a chance when he didn't have to. With Benefit aboard, she had credibility, so other brands signed on, and soon she had a solid list of partners.

She views success as a self-fulfilling prophecy, meaning that things you believe to be, come to be. Believing is what makes them happen.

In their Harvard apartment, she and Hayley stuffed two hundred sample boxes. These would be the **beta test** boxes, the ones that would prove or disprove their business concept. (When testing things, the larger the sample, the less likely that one single reaction or opinion will skew the result. Two hundred is a solid beta sample.)

They used smart **networking** to recruit their testers. That means not sending to friends and family (investors wouldn't take that seriously) and instead finding "nodes" in the community—people who interact with lots of people, like lawyers and store owners—and asking those nodes to share the beta test with their friends. Well, it worked. Birchbox had so much interest they needed a huge waiting list. The trial proved people loved the idea.

> **Tip:** Going into business with a friend or partner is TRICKY. Up front, have lots more clarifying conversations than you'd ever imagine needing. What are your exact roles? What do you each do best? Who reports to whom? What happens if one of you wants to leave?

Now into the adolescent phase of Birchbox's development, Katia says the hardest thing about being CEO is that the minute she figures things out, the job changes. "As soon as you feel on solid ground, you need to do the next thing that's ill defined and impossible," she says. First Katia had to be a sales shark, signing up every brand she could. Then a pitch queen, dazzling investors in every room. After that, a hiring dervish. Then Hayley left, so she had to adjust to ruling solo. (This happens frequently in partnerships, including at Rent the Runway, Pals, Stitch Fix, Coolhaus, and Wildfang. Having two people at the top, especially friends, can be hard because of different styles and expectations and power dynamics.)

Last year, her job transformed again, to the toughest challenge yet: steering through extreme turbulence. A key business assumption was that after sampling a trial-sized dry shampoo or lotion, customers would click to buy a regular-sized amount. But often they didn't. Or they didn't buy it at Birchbox.com. Katia had to lay off many employees, cut **expenses,** and rethink the basic business model. Initially, she tried to sell the whole company to Walmart and QVC. Then she secured a $15 million investment, which saved Birchbox in a certain respect, but the deal was constructed in such a way that her other early investors did not end up making money. Still, Katia wasn't folding. Forget that. And good thing, because then along came Walgreens, who put money into the business and partnered to create Birchbox pop-ups inside their drugstores, where customers can test a Birchbox-curated assortment of cosmetics (and sign up for the subscription service). "Ninety percent of the game is that you stay in it," Katia says.

In their Harvard apartment, she and Hayley stuffed two hundred sample boxes.

For much of 2018, all of Katia's decisions were made from the horizontal position. Pregnant with her fourth child, she was put on months of hospital bed rest due to complications. Having children has sharpened her view that the fight for workplace equality must center on the return to work after giving birth. Improved maternity leave policy has been the demand of women, but the return to work, in Katia's mind, is when careers implode. Mind-sets and policies need shifting. "Women come back as a discounted asset. 'Oh, she needs flexibility.' 'Oh, let's not overburden her,'" Katia says. "Women didn't come to work to be stuck in midlevel management."

She intends to model a different storyline. "I am in such a unique and blessed position to try to change the narrative a little bit. I will not squander this opportunity. I am going to stay in the game and swing for the fences," she says.

EMILY WEISS

FOUNDER AND CEO OF
GLOSSIER

Business 101: Give your customers what they
want. Know by asking.

HER BUSINESS: A makeup brand for girls of all ages that looks to customers to shape their products.

SPEAKING UP STARTED EARLY: In high school, Emily wrote a letter to
the editor of *Vogue,* thanking her for a stellar fashion spread showing
how to wear a short skirt well. The letter made it into the magazine!

PLAYGROUND SHE'S IN: The $380-billion beauty industry.

MAKEUP FACT: The average woman spends $15,000 during her life-
time on beauty products, $3,000 on mascara alone, according to *Peo-
ple* magazine.

WEARING THE INSIDE OUT: Even though she's from New York, a place
famous for sidewalks full of people always in a rush with no patience
for pleasantries, Emily smiles when she walks down the street.

Glossier's showroom in New York City is a pink dream. Staff in pink mechanic-inspired jumpsuits and white sneaks (no socks) circulate

Tip: With the boom in online shopping, in-person retail needs to be an extra-special experience. Create something unique that thrills the senses and gives lots of opportunity to try the products.

with iPads, noting shoppers' choices, which they then gather and deliver in pink translucent bags. The walls are the same cotton-candy pink as Glossier's adorable boxes. There are pink orchids and bunches of pink roses. The blush, all shades perfectly lined up on little raised displays, looks utterly photo-worthy, which is, of course, by design (the hashtag #glossierpink now has 18,024 Insta posts).

This makeup brand has become a cult favorite among girls and young women. There are lines around the block to enter the NYC shop. At one point, Glossier's Boy Brow eyebrow pomade (about which they advertise, "Brush your teeth, brush your brows, and then maybe brush your hair") sold out and had a ten-thousand-person waiting list. Emily, the company's CEO, has said in the press that Glossier makes more money per square foot at its New York shop than the average Apple store. That's a lot of eighteen-dollar Stretch Concealer and Lidstar eyeshadow.

Like RewardStyle and PopSugar, Glossier began with a wee-hours-of-the-morning blog. While working as a stylist's assistant at *Vogue,* Emily woke daily at four a.m. to update *Into the Gloss,* her now-famous beauty blog, which she started in 2010. Launching the blog cost her about $1,000, including $700 for a digital camera. Her *Vogue* job included hanging around with supermodels and fashion designers, and she was always asking them lipstick this and hairdo that, which gave her the idea to demystify the beauty routines of the famous and fabulous. On *Into the Gloss,* she took her readers inside these fashion professionals' makeup bags and bathroom drawers and revealed their daily routines and beauty insecurities. She knew women would really bond if they all got a little vulnerable and shared what bugs them about their looks. She had a knack for getting people like supermodels Karlie Kloss and Bella Hadid and Spice Girl–turned-entrepreneur Victoria Beckham to spill all.

Over a few years, the blog grew to have 10 million monthly views. The intense interest gave Emily an idea. The beauty industry didn't have any brands that she felt matched the current moment. Buying makeup meant surviving intimidating, overly made-up department store counter attendants all trying to sell you a million products you didn't need and would never use in real life, and feeling like all questions were idiotic. Being way savvy about lip liner was equally problematic, because beauty is superficial and anyone who cares too much must be shallow. Those were the two extremes Emily experienced. She thought, *You can't win!* But what if she completely reinvented the cosmetics experience? She would get her blog followers to tell her what makeup products they *really* wanted.

While working as a stylist's assistant at Vogue, *Emily woke daily at four a.m. to update* Into the Gloss, *her now-famous beauty blog.*

Her idea was still vague, but Emily decided to go talk to some investors about starting a dream makeup brand built around customers' ideal products. She drove up and down a famous road near Stanford

University called Sand Hill Road, where lots of venture capitalists have offices. Her rental car was full of boxes of samples, and she stood in the parking lot and picked and packed an array to take inside to her meetings with the VCs. Basically everyone she met was male, so the samples went to their wives, girlfriends, or assistants. Her first ten meetings turned up ten nos. Then one VC said he liked her idea, but it was too "early-stage" for him (meaning she should come back to him when she had a clearer plan and some customers). He suggested she call Kirsten Green at Forerunner Ventures, then an all-female-held fund. The moment Kirsten met Emily, she knew she needed to work with her. Kirsten once told a reporter, "Emily is my best case study in having a gut instinct on somebody."

> **Tip:** Good things come to people who ask. If you don't push for something, no one is going to just imagine you want it and go to the trouble of making it happen. It starts with networking and then asking the people you meet for what you want. Graciously, of course.

Emily has been a go-getter all her life. She credits her dad with teaching her that plain old hard work is the secret to everything. He never finished college and worked his way up from salesman at postage-meter manufacturer Pitney Bowes. There's clearly some of him in her. At age fifteen, when she was in high school and a "theater nerd," she was babysitting for some kids in her town of Wilton, Connecticut, and one of the parents worked at Ralph Lauren corporate in New York City. Emily got gutsy and said, "I love your kids, but what I'd really like is for you to introduce me around your office and help me get hired as an intern." They did, and she worked there for two summers.

She was a standout in her appearance (she modeled briefly), but more importantly, she was tenacious in her work ethic, always going above and beyond in her intern tasks. One of her mentors at Ralph Lauren got her in front of the editor of *Teen Vogue,* who invited her to intern there next. Emily crammed her classes at NYU into two days so she could spend three days interning at the magazine. Later, she worked at MTV, where she briefly appeared in the reality show *The Hills* as a type-A super-intern (which is just what she was!).

Tip: If you manage to get in the door, don't blend into the woodwork and passively wait to be told what to do. Be upbeat, self-starting, assertive, and such a hard worker that you can't help being noticed.

From *Teen Vogue* she graduated to *Vogue,* where she went from intern to style assistant. Always giving more than expected, standing out, always in the right place at the right time to hear the gossip that would fill the pages of her blog, which would lead naturally to Glossier.

Glossier launched on Instagram with 15,000 followers before a single mascara wand was even for sale. That was no accident. Social media is in Emily's DNA. She understands its powers and how to use them. Exhibit A: When she took the time to create the intricate line drawing with leaves and flowers and a pineapple wearing sunglasses framing a unique graphic *G* for the label of the Mega Greens Galaxy Pack mask and shared it on her social media channels, she knew her followers would snap a shot and post it everywhere, which they did. Exhibit B: She features real customers, found through social media, in Glossier's ad campaigns. In fact, someone at the company

has the job of scrolling through Insta photos and direct messaging gals who have "the look" to come on out to New York City to join up (sounds like a fun job, right?).

About six weeks after the website launched, the VC who had previously felt Glossier was too early-stage for his money made a big investment. Now, with $8.4 million, Emily invested in technology and data analytics to study Instagram and other social platforms, measuring how well certain Glossier posts performed and which Glossier products got customers snapping photos and posting. She launched her blush called Cloud Paint on the red carpet at the Oscars. Ten makeup artists put the blush on celebrity clients attending the awards night and then posted the results on social media. Four weeks later, there were 6,368 images of Cloud Paint on Instagram.

To create the first products, Emily partnered with a chemist in California. She launched with just four products—cleanser, moisturizer, lip balm, and mist. Today she is up to forty products, with new ones released every six to eight weeks. She takes a lot of feedback from customers, always asking online whether shades are too blue or too orange, and listening hard. Emily once asked her Glossier followers what they want in a moisturizer, and she got one thousand responses.

A big problem has been constantly running out of stock of favorites, thus disappointing clamoring customers. Emily prefers to go straight to her fans with an honest explanation and apology. She posted on *Into the Gloss,* "Building a company is a little like going through puberty— we're growing up, which is cool, but sometimes it's a bit awkward." She says getting the right ingredients in the right formulation with the right feel "often means many rounds of testing, followed by long lead times (up to eight months!) between batches." Lucky for Emily, basic consumer psychology is such that an out-of-stock message often leads buyers to want it even more—clearly, it's sold out for a reason!

She launched her blush called Cloud Paint on the red carpet at the Oscars. Ten makeup artists put the blush on celebrity clients attending the awards night and then posted the results on social media.

In her Manhattan company headquarters—which is 79 percent female-staffed and where conference rooms are named after women the team admires, like singer Rihanna and model Kate Moss—Emily uses an internal texting program called Slack, which a lot of businesses use to communicate among employees. There are different channels, each for an individual topic. One channel Emily created is called #kudos. It's a place where people give each other credit for doing great work.

The Glossier crew should be giving each other lots of #kudos. In 2018, Glossier expanded into Europe, surpassed $100 million in sales, and become a beloved hot brand. Then, in 2019, Glossier was valued at over one billion dollars! Yes, #kudos all around!

FLOWERS

CHRISTINA STEMBEL

FOUNDER, CEO, AND GRUNTSWOMAN OF
FARMGIRL FLOWERS

Business 101: Embrace necessary change (even, sometimes, change to your company mission).

HER BUSINESS: Bouquets of seasonal flowers ordered online, wrapped in trademark burlap, and delivered by bike or truck.

VERY FIRST JOB: Detasseling corn (taking the tops off corn plants before harvesting to allow for better growth) for $2.25 an hour at age eleven.

A WEIRD THING YOU'LL FIND ON (OR IN) MY DESK: Usually some gloves, so I can strip flowers and not get covered with eucalyptus sap.

HIGH SCHOOL GPA: Around a 3.0.

WORST SUBJECT IN SCHOOL: Math. I hate fitting into the negative stereotype that girls are bad at math. Girls can be GREAT at math!

MY BEDTIME: One or two a.m.

ON MY BUCKET LIST: Get my pilot's license. And get back to riding motorcycles. I have carpal tunnel syndrome from working with flowers (a few years ago I was still doing eighty to one hundred bouquets every day), so first I need to go to physical therapy and then I'll go back to motorcycles.

A GUILTY PLEASURE: Fake eyelashes so I don't have to wear eye makeup.

FAVORITE CANDY: I'm not a candy person, but I like ice cream. This morning I had a bowl of chocolate peanut butter!

FAVORITE CHILDHOOD BOOK: *Anne of Green Gables.*

FAVORITE FLOWER: *Everyone* asks! Peonies—specifically tree peonies that are as big as my face—king protea, and blooming jasmine (nothing smells better).

HOW OFTEN I CHECK MY BANK STATEMENT: Three times a day. I also check my credit card processing and my credit card statement.

A TOOL I ALWAYS WANT TO HAVE IN MY HOUSE: Floral shears. I'm always taking home flowers to do Instagram pics on weekends, and my kitchen scissors are not ideal.

WORDS TO LIVE BY: It's naive to think I learn everything from just research. Some things you can only learn by doing.

Christina's business philosophy is inspired by one of her all-time-favorite places: In-N-Out Burger. They laser focus on one thing (for them, the basic burger) and make it *exceptional.* She aims to do the same with her bouquets. Instead of selling hundreds of different bouquets every day, Farmgirl Flowers just sells a handful, but boy, are those EXCEPTIONAL. For years, she offered just one arrangement daily, using only the most in-season buds. She needed fewer staff, because assembly was simpler. Most important, she could calculate exactly how many flowers she needed, which meant almost zero buds tossed.

Christina is a true farm girl. She grew up in Indiana, the great-granddaughter, granddaughter, and daughter of soybean and corn growers. So she cares deeply about farmers—American ones particularly. Researching the floral industry, she discovered that most flowers come from faraway places like Ecuador and Holland, traveling thousands of miles on airplanes, then refrigerated trucks, wasting gas all the way. But because they grow on huge industrial farms and are sold in bulk, prices

Tip: Examining your childhood and family history is a great place to look for problems that move you deeply enough to start a business to solve.

stay low. Because of these realities, between 1976 and 2000 around 60 percent of American growers left the business. Christina's founding mission was to revitalize American growers. She'd do for flowers what farmers' markets do for food—provide eco-friendly, small-batch, and local bouquets.

Before launching Farmgirl, Christina worked in donor events at Stanford University. For fancy lunches, she'd pay $200 for a giant floral centerpiece (tacky-looking, at that!) from a traditional florist. They were expensive because 40 percent of flowers purchased by florists end up in the trash without ever making their way to a bouquet. Because they offer so many different arrangements, florists never know exactly how many of each flower they need, and lots of flowers go to waste. In better news, only once in Farmgirl's history has the company ever wasted more than 1 percent of their flowers.

Christina started Farmgirl Flowers in 2010, purchasing her stems from the San Francisco Flower Mart in the wee hours of morning and arranging the bouquets in her teeny San Francisco apartment. Her bathtub was crammed with buckets of flowers, petals everywhere. She followed web tutorials ("I graduated from the University of YouTube," she jokes) and received online orders late into the evening. In 2012, her apartment landlord booted her out because running a business from the building was illegal. Instead, she rented a stall at the Flower Mart and hired a fleet of bike messengers to pedal her floral arrangements around town in baskets.

Christina is a true farm girl. She grew up in Indiana, the great-granddaughter, granddaughter, and daughter of soybean and corn growers. So she cares deeply about farmers—American ones particularly.

Even today, Christina is still hands-on. Her business card says FOUNDER, CEO, AND GRUNTSWOMAN, and on a recent holiday, her Fitbit logged twenty-six miles as she ran around the warehouse.

Christina used $49,000—every dollar of her savings—to start Farmgirl. She quit her event co-ordinator job at Stanford to focus on her business full-time. She knew having no other income would propel her to action. That first leap was terrifying, though, especially for a single gal living on her own. But she worked her butt off and saved money wherever she could. She even quit coffee because tea bags cost much less. For publicity, she brought flowers to cafés around town and offered a free bouquet in exchange for a promise to display them up front. She would put a stack of cards beside them. If fifty or more cards were gone when she returned, she considered that café locale worth the twenty dollars the flowers cost.

But her coolest marketing idea yet may be her trademark burlap wrap, which holds her flowers instead of a vase. Christina called up a coffee roaster nearby and offered to take used bean sacks off their hands. She cut them up and folded the bits like taut baby blankets around the stems. The burlap made people recognize the flowers as Farmgirl, the same way the swoosh screams Nike or the red wax casing gives away Babybel cheese. In fact, on one memorable evening delivery in 2014, with only $411 left in her bank account and real fear that Farmgirl was near failing, three women stopped her. "Oh my gosh, are those Farmgirl?" they gushed. They recognized the burlap! That was the moment Christina started believing her brand actually meant something. As it happened, the burlap was so supercool other florists copied her. She had trademarked "burlap-wrapped flowers," but a judge ruled that "flowers wrapped in burlap," as her competitor advertised, was okay. She now tries to think of all the knock-offs as compliments.

By the end of her first year, she'd made $56,000 in **revenue.** By year three, with a boost from Facebook and Yelp advertising, she'd earned $920,000. But she still went five years without taking a salary, choosing instead to invest all the money back into her growing business.

Christina treats Farmgirl like her own baby, and she considers any problem that arises her problem (this explains her 120-hour work weeks). When customers began complaining about blemished flowers, she acted like a sleuth to uncover the issue. Normally, Farmgirl had almost no bad write-ups, so what was the problem? She followed some test flowers from their arrival at the shop, through boxing and shipping, to the delivery at her friends' houses. She discovered that since switching warehouses, the giant carts of flowers were being pulled over a speed bump when traveling to the arranging area. Water in the buckets was sloshing out, getting on the flower heads and causing brown spots. She changed the cart routing, and voilà, conundrum solved.

Of course, Christina tracks Farmgirl's numbers like a hawk. She looks at her credit card and bank statements several times a day. "Every weekend I send an email to the team, asking, what are these charges I don't recognize?" she says. "Like forty dollars to a hardware store, which turned out to be new blades for the burlap cutter." She's careful because she "bootstrapped" Farmgirl Flowers, meaning she built the business using only her savings and company earnings—she didn't have investors.

Growing up, Christina was continually spouting invention ideas (iron-on pockets for pocket-less clothes was a favorite until she decided . . . nah). As a high schooler she worked two fast-food jobs, regularly opening at Arby's and closing Burger King the same day. "I always smelled like a French fry," she says. From a young age, she knew she would leave Indiana and her very religious household. Her parents didn't think girls needed college, because they would just marry and be supported. A great regret of hers remains not arguing and getting a college degree. Christina moved to New York City right after high school. There, she worked three jobs. A massive splurge for her was eight-dollar baked ziti, which she stretched into two meals.

All that hard work gave her the most important skill of all—perseverance. She just keeps pushing through every barrier. To expand the company, she needed to sell to the whole country. But delivery is very expensive. Eventually Christina would build distribution centers dotting the country, which would solve this problem (the flowers would be close to the customers, wherever they were), but she is just now building her first distribution center on the East Coast. So she needed a short-term solution. She would pay for all shipping, which would badly cut into profits, so that her bouquets could go places like Charleston and Chicago but not become so pricey no one would order them. She had the determination to take this hard but necessary step for the business. Happily, she still managed to make $14.5 million in profit in 2018.

Tip: Oftentimes you need to be willing to give up some profit in the short term to make the money in the long term. Make those sacrifices with a smile.

One problem she couldn't solve was how to keep her pledge to buy from US growers exclusively as her company grew bigger. Her fast growth put a strain on her suppliers, and then California legalized marijuana. Many flower farmers instantly tore out their crops to lease their greenhouses to marijuana growers, happy to earn $1.50 per square foot versus $0.05 for flowers. She also found that US farmers didn't grow the variety of flowers she wanted to include in her bouquet. For years she tried to find ways to keep her pledge, but in 2018, she was forced to add non-US growers to stay in business. She was beside herself, but she handled this problem as best as she could by writing her customers an honest explanation. A tiny concession: She still offers one arrangement that she calls "Grown in the US of A," and she guarantees just that.

Upbeat, bloomin' news keeps coming, though. She's selling about 4,500 bouquets weekly. On Mother's Day week in 2018, she shipped 28,000! She has started building more critical distribution centers, her bike couriers receive full benefits (including health care), and she partnered with Rent the Runway (page 3) to make chic corsages for rental prom dresses.

She's selling about 4,500 bouquets weekly. On Mother's Day week in 2018, she shipped 28,000!

People constantly ask Christina for her quick advice. "No such thing," she says on her website. "Just like money doesn't grow on trees—secret sauce isn't packaged in a cute little bottle."

STATIONERY

MARIAM NAFICY

FOUNDER AND CEO OF

MINTED

Business 101: Hidden talent is everywhere. Find it.

HER BUSINESS: A marketplace that finds top artistic talent through design contests, then produces and sells that talent's greeting cards, invitations, fabric, party supplies, and fine-art prints (paying the artist a portion).

A WEIRD THING YOU'LL FIND ON (OR IN) MY DESK: *The Elements of Typographic Style.* A truly nerdy book about type.

HIGH SCHOOL GPA: Around 3.3. When I moved back from Egypt in high school, my grades plummeted. I was really depressed and was getting Cs and Ds. I did rebound.

SOMETHING THAT DRIVES ME CRAZY: People who prefer complaining to offering solutions.

A GUILTY PLEASURE: French fries and bad TV, specifically *Naked and Afraid.*

FAVORITE CANDY: Candy corn.

FAVORITE CHILDHOOD BOOK: *The Lion, the Witch and the Wardrobe.*

SOMETHING I WISH I HAD INVENTED: There's so many things. Spanx (page 11).

FAVORITE PART OF MY JOB: Suggesting an employee try something new and watching them learn and grow and succeed in that new thing.

ADVICE I'D GIVE TO MY THIRTEEN-YEAR-OLD SELF: You are overly worried. It's all going to turn out just fine.

Picture yourself prepping madly for a homemade fudge sale. You have labored since dawn perfecting three delectably chocolaty and chewy varieties, all now cut and ready to serve. Your table is glitter decorated, your trays piled high. You hang a hand-drawn sign and declare yourself open for business. Then . . . NOBODY shows up. Not a single treat eater buys a single stinkin' fudge chunk. Replace the fudge with paper, and you pretty much have the beginning of Minted.

The tale begins in 2007. Mariam signed up a bunch of well-known stationery brands to sell their cards, letterhead, invitations, and more on her new online paper store. She asked angel investor friends for a few thousand dollars, had a developer build her a simple website, and announced the Minted grand opening. She was proud of her business idea and its name, which a branding agency had helped brainstorm. (They asked her: If your company ideal is "clean" and "fresh," what are foods and plants that share those qualities? Cucumber . . . sprigs of basil . . . mint. Mmmm, mint. Minty. Minted!)

But the name couldn't save her. Opening day came and went and not a single box of Minted stationery sold. Same thing on day two. And three. Day thirty came and went, and now she had opened a business with zero sales in the first month. "It was frightening. It was puzzling . . . downright depressing. I thought, Maybe this is just a fail. Maybe I pull the plug and give all the money back," she says.

It didn't help that many people she trusted had told her Minted was a bad idea, including a prestigious Stanford professor whose opinion she valued. Stationery would never sell online, he insisted.

But what stressed her out most—maybe even more than losing every penny of her funder friends' money—was how this would look to those critics who were already skeptical of her early career success. In 2000, at age twenty-seven, she'd founded the very first online makeup retailer, Eve.com, and sold it for $110 million before her thirtieth birthday. Because that all happened so fast, and she was a complete newbie, onlookers (some surely jealous) cried, "Beginner's luck!" Ever since, a certain nasty phrase had lodged itself in her brain: *Once you're lucky, twice you're good.* Mariam definitely didn't want to be lucky. She wanted to prove she could repeat success.

> **Tip:** Thomas Edison's light bulb was mocked. Communications execs told Alexander Graham Bell his telephone was "hardly more than a toy." A radio pioneer called TV "a development of which we need waste little time dreaming." Same for cell phones, airplanes, computers . . . There will always be haters. Don't let them poison your positivity.

Really, she already had. When she was ten, her family fled to America to escape the Iranian Revolution. She learned a new language in pretty much an instant, then immediately jumped ahead, skipping two grades. Her mom was a major influence. In first grade she told Mariam,

Tip: If you get rejected, wallow for one minute, and then look up and ask yourself, *What can I do to change the next outcome, or make myself a stronger candidate, or ace the next interview?*

"I want you to go beat all the boys." Mariam, meanwhile, was thinking, *What if we had never been able to leave Iran?* These twin forces—ambition and an appreciation of her good fortune—turned Mariam into an unstoppable engine. The word *no* didn't register. When her first application to Stanford business school was rejected, she didn't sulk; she asked admissions how she might improve her chances. "Stand out more," they said. So Mariam, then twenty-six years old, wrote a book—*The Fast Track: The Insider's Guide to Winning Jobs in Management Consulting, Investment Banking, and Securities Trading*—about her years working on Wall Street. She reapplied, and Stanford said, "Welcome!" She paid for much of business school with her book advance.

The rejection continued. Right out of Stanford, Mariam founded a business with a close friend. When the domain Eve.com wasn't available—it'd been taken by a little girl named Eve—Mariam and her partner didn't ditch their desired name; they doubled down. They showered little Eve with free Disneyland trips and money until she gave up the domain. Within six months, they had 120 employees and comfy offices, and by the end of the year, they had $10 million in sales.

Ever since, a certain nasty phrase had lodged itself in her brain: Once you're lucky, twice you're good.

But now Minted's failed start was all Mariam saw. The terrible visitor stats might spell company doom. She wondered how not to hear "no."

Unsure of how to plow ahead, she allowed herself to pursue a unique contest idea that had been brewing in her brain for a while. It was definitely off strategy from selling brand-name stationery, but she decided to at least try because she badly needed something to reinvigorate Minted. So nightly, after office hours, Mariam sat in her tiny San Francisco apartment and worked remotely with a Portland, Oregon, computer wiz she hired on Rent-acoder.com to create a tool that would enable design competitions on the Minted website. Her idea: to motivate independent designers to upload amazing cards that Minted customers could then vote on. The favorites would get produced and sold. And the artists who designed them would make a percentage of the sales. So if the top-pick holiday card set sold for $30, the designer got approximately 15%, or $4.50 ($30 × .15 = $4.50).

Mariam had an instinct that one of the unexplored values of the internet was the ability to provide a powerful new platform for unearthing hidden talent. The concept had a name: **crowdsourcing.** By inviting everyone everywhere—even doodlers in Dubuque, stone carvers in Greece, and grandmas in Argentina—to submit designs and possibly make money, there was a great chance of finding undiscovered talent. "Creativity can come from anywhere," Mariam likes to say. This little *side* project quickly became the *main* idea.

The first Minted card competition attracted a respectable sixty entries. Soon, thousands of entries were pouring in, from Trinidad, South Africa, New Zealand, and beyond, and the best-selling cards on Minted were all contest winners.

Mariam wasn't just lucky after all.

It turned out her great idea just required an adjustment—a creative design competition—to give it life. Evolution like that is constant, says Mariam, even long after launch. Like in December 2013, when Minted's biggest card-selling competitor called to say, in short, "Sorry, just warning you that we are buying the printer that produces half of your inventory." The competition knew it couldn't win over Minted's customers, so it was trying a new tactic: cut off the paper supply. Evil but smart. Within hours, Mariam's team was racing around the country hiring new printing companies to complete their jobs.

Her mom was a major influence.
In first grade she told Mariam, "I want you
to go beat all the boys."

Mariam calls that period "Printergeddon," after the biblical term Armageddon, which refers to an end-of-the-world scenario. But they survived. Today Minted is crushing it. They have expanded the contest concept to home decor and fine-art prints. They sell hundreds of millions of dollars worth of well-designed goods.

Mariam is pretty proud of herself. She's definitely beating the boys, as her mom directed her to, and she's talking about it, too. In fact, one of her new missions is pushing girls to brag more about all their awesome feats at #shebrag. "Why is it that the average talented woman doesn't engage in the same truth-amplifying braggadocio that the average man does?" she posted recently. Yeah, why? Mariam says, "Let's start now and #shebrag together."

APPS/TECH

MACI PETERSON PHILITAS

COFOUNDER AND CEO OF
ON SECOND THOUGHT

Business 101: Sometimes the best ideas are the most obvious ones.

HER BUSINESS: A technology giving texters a grace period to take back that rude/wrong/mean message they just sent.

VERY FIRST JOB: Babysitting.

A WEIRD THING YOU'LL FIND ON (OR IN) MY DESK: A bottle of honey. I use it in my coffee.

HIGH SCHOOL GPA: 3.8.

WORST SUBJECT IN SCHOOL: Math.

AS A KID, WHAT I WANTED TO BE WHEN I GREW UP: A Baskets of Joy lady (custom gift basket biz my mom ran).

MY BEDTIME: Ten p.m., but I'm bad at sticking to it.

ON MY BUCKET LIST: Go to Antarctica.

A GUILTY PLEASURE: Watching *The Real Housewives of Atlanta*.

AN EXPRESSION I USE A LOT THAT PEOPLE KNOW ME FOR: #gogod

FAVORITE CANDY: I'm not into sweets.

FAVORITE CHILDHOOD BOOK: *Where the Wild Things Are.*

HOW OFTEN I CHECK MY BANK STATEMENT: Every day, at least once.

ADVICE I'D GIVE TO MY THIRTEEN-YEAR-OLD SELF: Don't worry so much about what others think of you. Honestly, it's something I still struggle with.

Maci Peterson's ex-boyfriend had been calling constantly, but she wasn't picking up. She was super busy; plus, she was trying to move on. Still, she hated being rude, so she finally texted him: *Sorry I keep missing your calls.* Three seconds later, glancing at her screen, she was mortified. Oh no! On her last word, she'd accidentally typed *b* instead of *c*. (You get the BIG problem, right?) What would he make of her message? Wasn't there some Harry Potter–esque magical spell she could conjure? If only there was a function on her phone to turn back time. . . .

> **Tip:** Google is your friend. Many of these entrepreneurs joke that they have a PhD in Google and YouTube. When you're stuck on how to get your idea started, start there.

The idea for On Second Thought hatched there. A way to take back texts was such an obvious idea she couldn't believe no one had invented it already. She googled and googled but found nothing. She searched the US Patent and Trademark Office database but found nothing. Were others as desperate for this as she was? She emailed thirty or forty friends, asking how often they were embarrassed by autocorrect screwups related to boyfriends or otherwise, or had angry-texted and regretted it. The responses all came in the same: every day, basically.

With this hot idea burning inside her, she saw a notice about a **pitch competition** at the South by Southwest tech fest happening in Austin, Texas. She quickly filled out the form on the website and was almost instantly accepted. Because everything was so last-minute, she had to take a standby flight and just made it to the competition. Luckily, the presentations were only one minute long, because she hadn't yet figured out any details beyond her basic idea. Really,

Tip: Pitch competitions are everywhere. Enter some! They are a great way to get noticed. The questions you get asked (especially the ones that stump you!) will help you improve your idea. Plus, you can win some moola.

she wasn't even sure her text-takeback concept was technically possible. After twenty wannabe entrepreneurs pitched the judges, they announced a winner. Drumroll . . . Maci Peterson, of On Second Thought!

Now she really had to figure out if her idea was technically possible. She had been living in Washington, DC, first selling advertising, then marketing for a *Washington Post*–owned publication called *The Root,* and then working in hotel management, and had built a network of young professionals. She started asking around. Everyone said her idea was cool but impossible. Impossible. *Impossible.* Her reaction: "How could it really be impossible? So many so-called impossible things happen every single day!" She started trying to figure out her product. First, she hired some coders in India, through a website with for-hire techies you could engage for a short-term project and work with online. "That was a nightmare," she says. It was hard to work remotely without ever meeting the coders. Then she reached out to a technically inclined ex-boyfriend (not the one she sent that regrettable text to!).

They put their heads together and brainstormed existing places where content is delayed or reversed. Oh, right! TV! Television networks use a delay for live TV, in case someone curses, or loses their pants, or something truly outrageous happens. So yes, this delay must be possible! "We knew then we didn't have to reinvent the wheel. We just had to slightly innovate," she says. Next, they called their friend Stewart, who was a true techie. Maci is not—she studied film and public relations at Chapman University in California. After nine months of tinkering, Stewart had a solution. By creating a way to stall texts for sixty seconds before truly sending them, mistakes could be caught. They filed a patent for "delay and recall of mobile communication."

Everyone said her idea was cool but impossible.

To get their app out, they simply uploaded it to Google Play (the app store for Android). Pretty soon they had 2,500 downloads. Then some of Maci's friends from her days working in journalism wrote stories. "We had a tsunami of media articles," she describes. On Second Thought was profiled in the *Washington Post* and in her hometown paper. She was on Fox's morning TV show. Within forty-eight hours, they had 25,000 downloads.

At this time, Maci was still working full-time for Marriott, in global marketing. When the press whirlwind hit, her office phone started ringing nonstop. She had to tell her boss what was up. He was awesome about it. "Just remember to tell the reporters that you work for Marriott," he joked. She was doing radio interviews from her cubicle. "I made this little PLEASE KEEP IT QUIET sign to hold up." When the app took off, she could no longer keep her day job. She quit Marriott.

Now her company really needed funding. How else would she pay rent? They needed to seize the momentum, and they needed to hire technical help. To start, Maci did two smart things. First, she went on LinkedIn and searched for anyone in her network who might be helpful. One person she called was an old *Washington Post* colleague. Then, when she contacted people, rather than ask for money, she asked if they'd be willing to read her business plan and offer feedback. Her *Washington Post* colleague was willing, and he called some of his investor friends for her.

> **Tip:** Raising money often starts with a relationship. Try asking for advice before money. This helps get the person invested in your idea and more comfortable with you.

But funding the company was tough. Maci applied twice to a famous program in Palo Alto, California, called Y Combinator, that helps hundreds of entrepreneurs turn their smart ideas into businesses and also helps to get those businesses some early funding. Disappointingly, she was rejected both times. That really stung because getting in is a true seal of approval, and a golden ticket to all the resources start-ups require—advice, connections, money. Maci had to dig deep to remain positive. "You hear 'no' a lot. The hard part is not allowing those nos to get to you. I just kept thinking, there are billions of people on this planet, so someone is going to tell me yes. I just have to find them," she says. Her dad helped her think this way. A long time back, when the magazine she tried to start in college failed, he'd told her to keep perspective. The failure was *the idea,* not *her.*

Tip: Learn not to take rejection personally. As Maci's dad taught her, it's the idea that is being rejected, not the person.

One trick Maci uses to keep believing is to think about the paths of inventors she admires. She loves Walt Disney and Conrad Hilton, founder of Hilton hotels. "One of them got evicted for not paying rent. Well, I haven't been evicted yet!" she says.

"The hard part is not allowing those nos to get to you. I just kept thinking, there are billions of people on this planet, so someone is going to tell me yes. I just have to find them."

Meanwhile, Maci has been staying open-minded about how to best grow her business. She knows she doesn't have everything figured out, and she's willing to keep evolving her idea. One shift in thinking is recognizing that an app alone doesn't begin to service all the ways that people would like to use her text-reversal technology. Some ideas came from customers. Several asked whether On Second Thought could fix mistakes made when sending money on sites like PayPal. What a great idea! Then a very large company approached her: "Could we pay to use your technology?" This kind of arrangement is called a **license.** They would "rent" Maci's invention and implant it in their own systems, and the users would never even know On Second Thought was involved. Maci decided yes. Licensing was a whole different business model, and she could use it to grow her company into something much bigger. So she shut down the app. How's the licensing going? "The big whales are starting to circle," she says.

STEPHANIE LAMPKIN

FOUNDER AND CEO OF
BLENDOOR

Business 101: Expect to encounter some skepticism and judgment—put on your armor and get out there.

HER BUSINESS: A "blind" recruiting app that hides job applicant information (like photo and name) to combat discrimination against women and minorities. The goal is to make hiring fairer, based on merit, not bias.

A WEIRD THING YOU'LL FIND ON (OR IN) MY DESK: An old-school floppy disk that tech media website *Recode* gave me for being one of the folks they think are awesome.

HIGH SCHOOL GPA: 4.375.

WORST SUBJECT IN SCHOOL: Social studies.

VERY FIRST JOB: Data entry for my mom's desktop publishing business.

AS A KID, WHAT I WANTED TO BE WHEN I GREW UP: An Olympic skier.

MY BEDTIME: One to three a.m.

ON MY BUCKET LIST: Have a baby.

A GUILTY PLEASURE: Watching documentaries about Serena Williams over and over.

FAVORITE CANDY: Anything dark chocolate and almonds.

FAVORITE CHILDHOOD BOOK: Everything Dr. Seuss.

HOW OFTEN I CHECK MY BANK STATEMENT: Twice a month.

ADVICE I'D GIVE TO MY THIRTEEN-YEAR-OLD SELF: It's hard to see the forest for the trees, but in the words of Dory (from *Finding Nemo*), "Just keep swimming, just keep swimming."

In 2015, Stephanie was attending an entrepreneurship summit at 1600 Pennsylvania Avenue, which, if you don't know, is the address of the White House. She was invited by President Obama, and on the day he spoke, she listened as if under a spell. He was boasting about the explosion in US tech innovation and all the exceptional young STEM talent. He quipped, "The next Steve Jobs might just be named Stephanie." Her eyes popped open wide. It was an otherworldly moment. *Am I dreaming?* she thought. Obama was *definitely* referring to her (well, she was pretty sure)!

What made that moment even more transformative: The White House is just a few miles from the impoverished southeast DC neighborhood where she had been raised—without a father, by a mother who'd at one point been homeless while pregnant with Stephanie. And yet, here was Stephanie *in a room with the president*. He'd said her name. Talk about a long journey over a very short distance.

Stephanie has her auntie Greta to thank for the push into tech. Greta was a math wiz who studied computer science and worked at Westinghouse Electric Company. Visiting Greta's home meant stepping into a thrilling world Stephanie would have no access to otherwise. She saw her first cell phone and CD player there. And most important, she saw a woman, her aunt, who adored her work and traveled the world to satisfy her curiosity.

"The next Steve Jobs might just be named Stephanie."

It was Aunt Greta who connected Stephanie with a nonprofit that trained kids in web development. Stephanie took to it. Fast. She was coding by age thirteen and understood full-stack web development by fifteen, meaning she could write code comprehensive enough to turn a concept into a working website. The nonprofit prepped her for the standardized computer science exams she needed to take for her college applications. She aced them.

Next stop was Stanford engineering, where her list of tech credentials kept on growing. After graduation she was wooed by Microsoft, where she spent five years working with big companies on IT (IT is short for "information technology" and describes the complicated infrastructure that allows computers and networks to store and process data). From there, she went on to MIT business school, where she studied entrepreneurship and innovation.

But back before she accepted the job with Microsoft, Stephanie applied for a "not very technical" (as she puts it) software engineering position with a Silicon Valley tech company. After eight—yes, eight—rounds of interviews, the recruiter told her she "wasn't quite technical enough." Stephanie was shocked. This made zero sense, given her résumé and experience. She'd expected to get a great offer, not to be ushered to the door, licking her wounds.

Her idea for Blendoor can be traced back to the indignities of that day. She was sure her qualifications had nothing to do with what happened. She was sure she wasn't hired because of the color of her skin.

After getting fired up, she started investigating how many minority candidates with the necessary qualifications failed to get the jobs they applied for. She read a study by the National Bureau of Economic Research showing that a "white-sounding" name (e.g., Emily or Greg) held the weight of eight additional years of experience relative to someone with an "African American–sounding" name (e.g., Lakisha or Jamal) when it came to callback rates after responding to an ad for a job.

She couldn't sit by and gripe any longer. She had to do something. She began building an app that uploaded résumés while hiding the candidate's name, gender, race, and photo, thereby forcing employers to assess qualification based on work history and references. She made sure the app matched job requirements with the candidates' skills, providing a number score to show the strength of the match (much like Netflix does with movie recommendations). Finally, she programmed the app to rank companies based on the diversity they achieved and how equally they paid people with different backgrounds. She designed the app with transparency in mind and shared everything she found with the public.

Today, giants of Silicon Valley including Google, Facebook, Airbnb, and Twitter are using Stephanie's Blendoor app in their hiring. They all say they want to solve the problem of too little diversity and to attack unconscious and unwanted bias. One of Blendoor's slogans is "The future of work is blind." Since launching in 2015, the company has facilitated more than three hundred hires.

But even this badly needed innovation and her gold-standard client list don't free Stephanie from facing bias herself, particularly when it comes to fund-raising. In fact, she deems fund-raising "the hardest thing I've ever done." Venture capital investors hardly ever see people who look like her. (Just thirty-four American black women have EVER raised upward of $1 million in VC funding.) A peer even suggested she hire a white cofounder to help break down the barriers. She found the comment both fascinating and depressing; two hundred years ago,

African Americans running successful businesses used this trick, hiring a white man or white family to act as the public face of their company. Had we really not grown beyond that?

Her take is that these funders assess companies much the same way people bet at the horse track. "It's pattern matching," she explains. "They look at what breed, jockey weight, and horse size has won before and then pick that one." Since they don't see entrepreneurs like her, it's safer to just say no. "I'm a penguin trying to pitch the construction of a beach resort. They [VCs] just don't see it."

After eight—yes, eight—rounds of interviews, the recruiter told her she "wasn't quite technical enough."

"I fear that there are many people in this world (including myself) who may never be able to reach their full potential, due to poverty, homophobia, sexism, racism, and many other isms," she reflected to a CNN reporter. But Stephanie plans to beat the odds. She pulls constant all-nighters (she power naps, she swears). She takes her Magic Bullet blender and bags of fresh veggies to work, and keeps her brain fueled with vitamin-packed mixes. She stays hands-on in product development even as she hires more staff. Her goal is to build a billion-dollar company—something that's never been done by a black female. If she succeeds, she'll be the Jackie Robinson of tech billionaires.

Luckily, as focused as she is on that goal, she still manages to have plenty of fun. "This is a marathon, not a sprint," she says. She plays flag football every Sunday (as the quarterback!). She loves doing Insanity, a guaranteed-sweat-drench cardio workout. She has attended the weeklong Burning Man festival in the Nevada desert, Carnival in Trinidad, and the celebrity-studded Sundance Film Festival in Utah. She has heli-skied in Alaska. On her thirtieth birthday, she was desperate to find a pal who would go skydiving with her. Unfortunately, she failed to convince anyone, so that remains on her to-do list. Care to join her?

SARAH LEARY

COFOUNDER AND VICE PRESIDENT, MARKETING AND OPERATIONS, OF
NEXTDOOR

Business 101: Sometimes the second time's the charm.

HER BUSINESS: Like Facebook but for neighborhoods, to connect, sell, hire, share, and warn each other about cat-eating coyotes and package thieves.

VERY FIRST JOB: Camp counselor.

A WEIRD THING YOU'LL FIND ON (OR IN) MY DESK: Puzzles. I like things I can do with my hands.

WORST SUBJECT IN SCHOOL: French.

MY BEDTIME: Midnight.

ON MY BUCKET LIST: Take a year off and teach or coach.

ALWAYS IN MY FRIDGE: A bottle of champagne. You never know when someone who needs celebrating is gonna come over.

A GUILTY PLEASURE: Reality TV. Anything on Bravo.

AN EXPRESSION I USE A LOT THAT PEOPLE KNOW ME FOR: "GSD" (Get *stuff* done—polite version.)

FAVORITE CANDY: Twizzlers.

FAVORITE CHILDHOOD BOOK: *The Giving Tree.*

HOW OFTEN I CHECK MY WEBSITE GROWTH: I haven't done it in fifty minutes—ha! Probably five times a day. If we're approaching a milestone, then even more.

A TOOL I ALWAYS WANT TO HAVE IN MY HOUSE: At twenty-two, my dad gave me a toolbox for Christmas. I treasure it.

IF A BARBIE WERE MADE OF ME, I'D BE WEARING: Something I can wear while riding a Vespa.

ADVICE I'D GIVE TO MY THIRTEEN-YEAR-OLD SELF: You want to be respected and then liked.

In the summer of 2011, Sarah and several coworkers had a regular 10 a.m. meeting. Their agenda was always the same. Sit around the conference table for hours. Try to think up a billion-dollar idea. When you think you have something, bat it around. Research it further. Feel skeptical. Lightly trash the idea. Kill it completely. Rinse. Repeat.

Sarah had spent 2009 and 2010 working nonstop to launch Fanbase, an online community built around love of college and pro sports. Investors had poured in millions. Initially, that idea had felt like a slam dunk. Sports fanatics are engaged fans, which makes for a very active online community. But as Sarah and her two cofounders, both of whom she'd met at her previous job, built a website and started trying to sign partnerships with sports leagues and athletes, the air started seeping out of the balloon. They aimed to be the go-to spot for fans to yak about Sunday's game and get last night's scores, but users seemed plenty happy with the sites they were already frequenting. Fanbase wasn't good *enough* to bother switching. Probably the biggest mistake was going deep into website development without testing out the idea with their intended audience. "I kept saying, I know this is not the next ESPN," Sarah recalls. "It was a sinking feeling."

Sarah was an all-American lacrosse player at Harvard, so she was used to being a champion. She couldn't handle the mediocre—at best—reception of Fanbase. "It's hard to work at something when you don't think you have a winner," she says. As a lacrosse goalie, Sarah withstood hard balls being constantly hurled at her head, so quitting was not in her personal playbook. But there was no choice but to give up on Fanbase. The site traffic hit 15 million users but then completely stopped growing. The pro leagues weren't offering exclusive content. This was a Fail with a capital *F*. "You need to be a painkiller, not a vitamin," Sarah says of business ideas that work. "I'm not even sure Fanbase was a vitamin. Maybe more like a really bad mint."

Sarah told her investors she was returning their money. Her investors said no. They said they were betting on the team, so the team just needed a new idea. That's when the 10 a.m. meetings began. Having ideas is easy. Having a unique, doable, for-the-masses idea is rare—purple-four-leaf-clover rare. They had a whole graveyard of concepts that came and went. First was Digital Droppings, an augmented reality concept (the same technology enabling *Pokémon GO*). Then came Need Feed, a network where people could post things they need and the community would respond. Nah and nah again. Neither satisfied the must-have bar for concepts that stick.

Having ideas is easy. Having a unique, doable, for-the-masses idea is rare—purple-four-leaf-clover rare.

Then at one of the 10 a.m. meetings, someone started griping about a pothole on his street. He said (paraphrasing), "If only all my neighbors would call and complain, maybe the city would fix this."

Zing! This was the spark for the team's BIG idea—an online network to connect neighbors so they can discuss potholes and political action and wild dogs and everything in between.

Tip: It's easy to get rattled by worry over how you'll ever become this massive national brand, like Starbucks on every block. The trick is to just get started in one locale. Remember, Starbucks began with one little shop, as did McDonald's, In-N-Out Burger, Jamba Juice, and basically every mega-success biz you know.

Sarah and her cofounders signed up a new director of engineering and were off and running. This was June. Sarah conducted a two-hundred-person survey asking friends if they knew their neighbors. Seventy-eight percent replied they wished they knew them better. "I remember I asked two hundred people because that's the number I could do free on SurveyMonkey," she says. Sarah did in-person interviews with neighborhood leaders. Soon she was bugging her engineer to build a test site. He shook his head. No way. "He said, 'I'm not writing a line of code until you get more customer feedback.'"

It was sound advice. "At Fanbase, we spent too much time building without getting feedback," she says, remembering the flop. To capture the feedback she needed, to discover the gaps and problems and traps she couldn't foresee, she and the team decided to invest in a trial neighborhood.

A friend of Sarah's near Palo Alto, California, agreed to let them attend his next neighborhood meeting to pitch making his neighborhood the first in the Nextdoor

> **Tip:** There is no substitute for in-person contact with customers. Loyalty and trust grows from human connection.

experiment. Sarah won over the neighbors with her spiel about the demise of borrowing cups of sugar and general neighborliness. It was fall 2011, and Halloween was a week away. Little did Sarah know, Halloween is *the* holiday that motivates neighborly bonding. This residential area was holding a parade and party, and suddenly everyone was joining the Nextdoor platform to offer a bin for apple bobbing or volunteer to bake pumpkin bread.

The neighbors felt more communal vibes than they had ever felt before, they would later say. They had plenty to talk about, and conversations kept sprouting and growing. This was **proof of concept**! This works! So Sarah pitched another neighborhood right near her experimental site. Then one in Seattle. "I'd ask every friend, 'Hey, can we use your neighborhood?'" she says. In each place, they tested new functionalities, like street maps and directories. Sarah traveled to these places. She was on hand to troubleshoot problems. "I was there fielding calls all week. When someone had a question, I'd say, 'I'm just down the street at the coffee shop. I'll come talk to you.' They trusted us because we were there." Her goal was to add one hundred neighborhoods before summer's end.

Within months, the team had twenty-five neighborhoods. The experiment was working. They committed to a name—Nextdoor (ditching Neighborly, their first effort at branding). And then: a hiccup. Midway through that first year, the site was plagued by significant technical difficulties, and engineers took it down for repairs. Instantly, the phone started ringing nonstop. "The site is down! I need it!" Neighbors from across the country relied on Nextdoor for information about garage sales, lost backpacks, excess backyard fruit. That day, phones ringing like crazy, "We knew," Sarah says. "We had something." This was the feedback her engineer said she needed, proof that they had crossed the must-have, critical-business test.

"He said, 'I'm not writing a line of code until you get more customer feedback.'"

The growth at Nextdoor has been furious since that day, with 190,000 US neighborhoods plus a plan to expand into Europe. "There is no

way to do this without getting dirt under your nails," says Sarah, looking back. "You don't come up with the brilliant insights at the white-
board. It's being in the game and adapting as you go. There is an
element of suspending disbelief, going on the journey and figuring
things out."

AMBER VENZ BOX

COFOUNDER AND PRESIDENT OF
REWARDSTYLE

Business 101: Help yourself—great. Enable an army of gals to make a living—brilliance!!!

HER BUSINESS: A platform enabling style bloggers to earn money from their fashion picks. When followers click to buy the trench or loafers being modeled, the blogger gets paid a cut of those sales.

VERY FIRST JOB: In eighth grade, my friends and I had a summer camp.

A WEIRD THING YOU'LL FIND ON (OR IN) MY DESK: Sour straws.

HIGH SCHOOL GPA: 3.2.

WORST SUBJECT IN SCHOOL: Probably science.

MY BEDTIME: Midnight.

ON MY BUCKET LIST: Visiting Iceland and Marrakech.

A GUILTY PLEASURE: Starbucks Java Chip Frappuccino.

FAVORITE CANDY: Sour straws. (No wonder they're on her desk.)

FAVORITE CHILDHOOD BOOK: *Goodnight Moon.*

ADVICE I'D GIVE TO MY THIRTEEN-YEAR-OLD SELF: Work as soon as possible in the field you love or think you might love. By the time I graduated college I had seen so many aspects of the fashion industry, I was years ahead of my peers.

Amber has been telling others what to wear since first grade. And people have been listening! She would call up her best friend and plan their outfits so they would be coordinated just like her idol twins Mary-Kate and Ashley Olsen. When Mary-Kate dyed her hair red in one movie, Amber did the same. She went back to blond for a while but "looked too much like a cheerleader," she says (which is funny, because she *was* a cheerleader!). Once Amber started blogging, she wanted to stand out. As a redhead, she looked unique, sophisticated, and cool. As she says, she could quit the spray-on tanning, let her face go pale, and as a redhead that worked. Plus, with the first name Amber, how could she have anything *but* red locks?

In fifth grade, Amber was asked to leave math class for knitting and vending scarves in the back row. By middle school, she made and sold vintage jeans that she'd turned into skirts; and she was always on style point, in her trademark outfit of Dr. Martens boots, Old Navy tee with the sleeves rolled up, and Lucky Brand jeans, a purple bottle of freesia-scented body spray stuffed in her back pocket. By high school, she had evolved to wearing black miniskirts and Steve Madden wedges and was carrying around a notebook filled with drawings of her dream clothing collection (she called it *VENZEL*). While at Southern Methodist University, she launched a jewelry line that, in time, pulled in $100,000 in sales, and she became a personal stylist for women who came into the high-end boutique where she worked part-time. Right after graduating, she became a clothing buyer at that shop, a job that morphed into her own personal-shopping business, serving fancy clients who'd drop thousands on the stellar outfits she picked out.

One thread winds through every endeavor Amber has ever pursued: her fashion obsession. Clothes have cast a spell over her, and their power never wanes. Even as president of a major online fashion empire, clothes still make or break her day. "If I'm speaking onstage and I love my outfit, it makes me more confident. On a trip, if I have some cool outfits, it's way more fun," she says.

On a recent day in Dallas, she stood before hundreds of adoring fashionistas—aka influencers now making bucks off the RewardStyle tech platform she created. Every year Amber brings these influencers to Texas for a weekend bash, with loads of selfie-perfect backgrounds for cool photo shoots. All her guests are style mavens like her, with thousands of followers on Instagram, Snapchat, and their personal blogs. They do daily fashion shoots and post the looks that their followers then buy. Then, voilà, Amber's platform rewards the influencers for each purchase they motivate. No wonder her annual Dallas weekend is a worship-Amber fest. For the 2018 event, she sported her favorite Kate Spade handbag, which is shaped like a swan. It was trademark Amber. At the time, she was also crushing on two other Kate Spade creations, a pineapple purse and a camel-shaped one made of wicker . . . with tassels.

In short, starting RewardStyle was a natural extension of what Amber had been doing all her life. But the idea to transform from personal shopper to fashion blogger to founder and president of a company that helps thousands of other people around the world make money off their fashion insights didn't spark until her boyfriend (now husband) inspired her. Baxter, with limited patience for all her talk of kitten heels and leather satchels, joked (lovingly), couldn't she find some other fashion trendsetters to converse with who actually cared about these topics?! It was enough to push her to launch her own fashion blog, *Venzedits,* in 2010. She was twenty-two.

Even as president of a major online fashion empire, clothes still make or break her day. "If I'm speaking onstage and I love my outfit, it makes me more confident. On a trip, if I have some cool outfits, it's way more fun," she says.

Audiences ate it up. Amber was soon whipping out postings of three daily outfits for her loyal followers, including style numbers, prices, and discount codes. Women would ooh and aah, and then go buy her picks. With this happening, the obvious next question was, why was she still dirt-poor, living in her parents' basement, and eating cereal for dinner? She was driving all those sales for companies, essentially free advertising for the clothing brands and retailers. Frustratingly, she wasn't sharing in any of the money being made.

It was on one cruddy beach day while vacationing with Baxter in Miami, forced inside a Starbucks by rain, that the pair sat down and hashed out a remedy. The solution would help Amber, of course, but more important all the many fashion bloggers who were being cheated out of payment for their talent. The concept they hatched was a technology platform connecting brands and retailers with fashion bloggers. When a fashionista at home was inspired to buy those fringed jeans an influencer was sporting, they could click a simple link embedded in the blog post, connect to the retailer, buy them, and that retailer would know to "thank" the recommending blogger with a check for a percentage of the purchase price. *Ka-ching!* Enabling this was a win-win for everybody involved.

Amber sketched her idea for a website interface on a napkin. She and Baxter were so excited, they registered the website domain name RewardStyle on his iPhone right then. Back home in Dallas, they worked with an engineer to build a site prototype. That simple first version of RewardStyle launched in 2011.

Today Amber has hundreds of employees all over the world—London, New York, Shanghai, São Paulo, Berlin. They have one goal: Help influencers, almost all of them women, make money off their good taste. RewardStyle has launched an army of women in business for themselves—more than thirty thousand in one hundred countries, actually. Whoa. The company has partnered with 4,500 retailers already and more than one million brands. A few RewardStyle influencers make as much as $1 million a year! Many make a living or good money from blogging. As a group, in 2018, RewardStyle influencers drove well over $1 billion in retail sales.

But they were just getting started. Amber and Baxter had a huge innovative breakthrough in 2017, with the LIKEtoKNOW.it button they invented. (They spent a few days brainstorming, holed up in their permanent canvas tent, called a yurt; it's their getaway spot.) Their new tool was connected into then-exploding-in-popularity Instagram, where many of their influencers were doing the bulk of their posting, and customers were searching for fashion tips. An Instagram user could "like" an Insta post by a RewardStyle influencer, immediately triggering an email containing shoppable links for every product in the post. This made it simple for the shopper and, wonderfully, easy to tie purchases from a particular influencer to a retailer. The retailer then paid RewardStyle, who in turn paid the poster. They iterated LIKEtoKNOW.it until viewers could screen-shot an influencer's post anywhere it appeared—triggering that same email of shoppable links. More *ka-ching*!

Tip: Make time and space to think and create. If the day is a swirl of meetings, video calls, and text-a-thons, your brain isn't free to imagine breakthrough ideas. Find your secret hideout for alone time, and shhhh . . . don't tell anyone where you are!

Up until just before Meghan Markle married Harry, the newest English royal used RewardStyle to make her blog shoppable. Sadly, royal family rules forced her to shut it down after the couple said "I do." Emily Weiss (page 137) was on the platform, too, with her blog, *Into the Gloss,* before launching Glossier.

In a way, Amber and RewardStyle helped birth a new age of advertising. Instead of selling a look via an ad in a magazine, advertisers now turn to real people to sell goods; they've discovered that shoppers want the things their favorite influencers adore. Suddenly brands are courting these influencers, even sending them to Paris and Tahiti, and giving them cool new fashion to wear.

It's a lot of running around for Amber, too. Since founding RewardStyle, she's had three babies. The first one, Birdie, went everywhere Mom went (she's oh so stylish, often twinning with Amber, like sporting matching cat ballet flats from Charlotte Olympia), but the arrival of the next two made life more complicated. All the kids stay home when Amber travels now, and when Amber is home, she is religious about leaving work by 5:30 p.m. so she can fit in some solid family time. "Every minute I'm late is one less minute I get to see them each night," she says.

Up until just before Meghan Markle married Harry, the newest English royal used RewardStyle to make her blog shoppable. Sadly, royal family rules forced her to shut it down after the couple said "I do."

How has she figured out her billion-dollar business with no business training? "I always hire people who are smarter than me," she says.

MEDIA

LISA SUGAR

FOUNDER AND PRESIDENT OF
POPSUGAR

Business 101: Turn your hobby into your work.

HER BUSINESS: A media channel with a global audience of 100 million, sharing the latest on fashion, celebrities, beauty, and more, and selling lots of fun related products.

A WEIRD THING YOU'LL FIND ON (OR IN) MY DESK: A mug with an illustration of Brian [her dear hubby] on it.

HIGH SCHOOL GPA: I was a solid B student. I had to work hard to get those Bs.

VERY FIRST JOB: Urban Outfitters in Washington, DC, folding jeans.

MY BEDTIME: I'm a night owl. Around eleven or midnight.

ON MY BUCKET LIST: To read more. I just read *Daisy Jones & the Six.*

A GUILTY PLEASURE: It really is candy.

FAVORITE CANDY: Probably candy cigarettes. I like the chalky taste.

AN EXPRESSION I USE A LOT THAT PEOPLE KNOW ME FOR: "Totally."

FAVORITE CHILDHOOD BOOK: Sweet Valley High series or The Baby-Sitters Club.

HOW OFTEN I CHECK MY SITE TRAFFIC: Every day. Every hour.

ADVICE I'D GIVE TO MY THIRTEEN-YEAR-OLD SELF: It's going to get better. You are so caught up in things that aren't going to matter *at all*, from looks to GPA.

Lisa is the poster gal for making work FUN. She spun her passion into her career, which is the *ultimate* feat. Now she has built a media empire—clothing and makeup businesses and 100 million monthly visitors and growing—mostly by dishing about celebrities, fashion, bands, hipster vacation spots, and all things cool, and, of course, by always getting killer scoops. *PopSugar* is like the juiciest *People* issue but digital, and updated with fresh stories and videos hourly.

At twenty-nine, Lisa started blogging about movie stars (Matt Damon was her heartthrob), TV shows, and everything Hollywood because she was obsessed with pop culture. She just couldn't help blabbing all she knew to anyone who would listen. Working at a hip ad agency in San Francisco—mostly on spreadsheets (tracking ad costs for clients)—was not scratching her creative itch, so she spent

Tip: Listen up—if you can make your hobby and obsession your paid job, you have won the Game of Life!

lunch breaks and late nights tap, tap, tapping away at her computer, weaving tales of her beloved stars' lives. She would then zing her posts around to her pals. Soon she had followers impatiently awaiting updates on *Sex and the City* episodes, Matt Damon sightings, and movie debuts.

Lisa's writing was magic and just what the world wanted to read. But the casual blog she started with—*PopSugar*—could only take her so far. Luckily for Lisa, in 2005, when her coding-wiz husband, Brian, saw her blogging like a banshee and "heard" her readers chanting "more, more, more," he quickly built her a robust website with room for expansion. Lisa herself then learned **HTML coding** so she could post her own articles and photos. She added categories—food, travel, beauty, career, fitness, parenting—to the new site, and it grew so fast that Brian decided to quit his job to help her keep pace. Within a year of those very first blog posts, *PopSugar* had 1 million followers.

Looking back on her childhood, it's a lucky thing that Lisa's parents were not strict about television or curfews. They let her stay up till all hours watching any and all late-night TV. This fueled the culture junkie inside.

After college, she interned at the TV show *Fox After Breakfast*. Working in TV was a dream, but getting a full-time gig proved impossible and she ended up in advertising, scheduling the slots on shows where the agency's ads would run. "Like most people in their twenties, I had a lot of crappy jobs. I had tears. I had terrible bosses. I was undervalued." She was close to a TV career working in advertising, but not close enough!

That's when the blogging started . . . and never stopped.

Walk into PopSugar headquarters in downtown San Francisco today and you can feel the joy. The joy of having found your calling. There's a gumball machine, a foosball table, and a corner for Ping-Pong. There are Sour Patch Kids and Hot Tamales on the reception desk—for the taking! (Lisa is a candy-holic, if you couldn't tell from her company name.)

Lisa is a bundle of energy with bouncy red hair and piercing blue eyes. She usually wears jeans and sneakers in the office because she walks to work every day and—news flash—bosses can wear whatever they darn well please! And, because she's the boss, she can do other things that might sound insane to the rest of us . . . like fly three thousand miles to New York for a haircut (because, she says, her guy is seriously the only one who knows what to do with her unruly curls!). I mean, why run a fashion-forward site if you can't share (a little) of the celeb flair?

While PopSugar began as a digital magazine, it's constantly growing new branches. The latest expansion is into retail sales: clothes, makeup, and the monthly Must Have box, a bonanza of Lisa's favorite new products that arrives at your door, often including makeup from Lisa's new line, Beauty by PopSugar. She's having a ton of fun with her new clothing line, too—a partnership with Kohl's department store. She and several members of her team just flew to Los Angeles to shoot a commercial featuring the line's high-rise skinny jeans, cropped faux-leather moto jacket, stripe-y tees, and more.

"I always tell our writers to imagine themselves as judges on a reality show, and if a celebrity were there, would they say whatever they are writing to his or her face?"

Lisa's business mantra, which is really her life philosophy, is simple: Work hard and play nice. The company culture reflects this. Lisa and her husband, Brian, have worked like crazy. They are not above doing grunt work, from assembling the office's Ikea desks to stuffing goody bags for events. When her team is glued to the TV, watching every minute of hours and hours of pre- and post-Oscar partying, who buys the snacks? Lisa, the boss! Speaking of the Oscars, Lisa has gone ten times. The first four times she was press, covering the event. Then she started attending as a guest, wearing a glam floor-length dress and walking the red carpet, like the stars.

Tip: Be one of the people who are not above any work task. You will set the tone for everyone and will earn a mountain of respect.

While PopSugar has pretty much perfected your daily must-know news, they have a strict rule to remain kind. The positive, upbeat, respectful tone is different from competitors like *People, Entertainment Weekly,* and *Us;* readers have noticed and rewarded Lisa with their loyalty. "I always tell our writers to imagine themselves as judges on a reality show, and if a celebrity were there, would they say whatever they are writing to his or her face?"

One trick Lisa teaches her writers when doing interviews with big celebs is to start gently with easy-to-answer questions, which allows you to build some connection and trust. Then you can start inching toward the more sensitive topics by asking slightly indirect, related questions, which might let the conversation meander more naturally into the juicy stuff but won't put the star on guard. So instead of asking, let's say, Chrissy Teigen, about friends Kim Kardashian and Kanye West directly, which would likely make her cringe and roll her eyes, she tells her writers to inquire about her books, and her recipes, and her husband and kids, and pretty soon her infectious, hilarious personality comes out, making great material for a story.

The trick to a great interview is getting people feeling comfortable.

Lisa and her writing staff have a list of no-no words and phrases for *PopSugar* articles and headlines—it's constantly being updated. Her writers must avoid clichés and overly trendy, overused expressions and slang. Some of the words-to-avoid of the moment: *hunk, amaze-balls, staycation, hubby, cray, totes or totes amaze, yasss, preggers, spring has sprung, make your jaw drop, blow your mind.*

The trick to a great interview is getting
people feeling comfortable.

Her three daughters are learning these lessons, too. They are the sun(s) Lisa's earth circles around. The middle one, Juliet, has her excellent curly red hair, too. "She's known what to do with her hair since she was nine!" Lisa said, marveling. Her oldest, Katie, was born right after PopSugar launched. She spent her early years going to the office with Lisa every day, instantly becoming the company mascot. Now she's a teen, and her whole class spent half a day on-site with PopSugar's tech team as part of a STEM activity. The caboose (kid number three) is Elle. Well, she's a mega force in a miniature package, running circles around Lisa, her sibs, and all the suns and planets!

In 2016, Lisa wrote a book to inspire her fans and show readers how she's done it. It was nerve-racking going on tour and speaking before hundreds of people (she doesn't seem it, but she swears she's kinda shy). She practiced with a coach, but even that made her nervous. One trick was having someone film her rehearsing her presentation so she could see her awkward habits. But the biggest challenge may have been the talk she gave on the morning of November 9, 2016, right after Donald Trump was elected. She had been at the Javits Center in New York City until the wee hours, blogging from Hillary Clinton's supposed-to-be victory party. She then had to race home, shower, and speak to an ad agency crowd about her book, *Power Your Happy: Work Hard, Play Nice, and Build Your Dream Life*. But she somehow found the right words. No surprise. Clearly, she has a knack for that.

> **Tip:** Try cleansing your vocabulary of clichés, trendy terms, and trashy jargon. Especially *like*. Erase *like* from your memory bank. Sayonara. When you start working in the real world, you'll be taken more seriously.

BEATRIZ ACEVEDO

FOUNDER OF
MITÚ

Business 101: Find an audience that has been overlooked.

HER BUSINESS: A media network, Mitú, focused on young Latinos, producing content for Netflix, YouTube, Facebook, and network TV.

VERY FIRST JOB: DJ at a radio station when I was eight years old.

WHAT I WANTED TO BE WHEN I GREW UP: A psychologist (just like my mom).

A WEIRD THING YOU'LL FIND ON (OR IN) MY DESK: Tajín (a spicy chili powder I put on anything).

WORST SUBJECT IN SCHOOL: Philosophy.

MY BEDTIME: Eleven-ish.

ON MY BUCKET LIST: Culinary school (preferably in Italy).

A GUILTY PLEASURE: Dessert.

AN EXPRESSION I USE A LOT THAT PEOPLE KNOW ME FOR: "Calladitas no more." ("Quiet no more!" A phrase I use a lot to encourage girls to speak up. But it goes against a lot of grandmas and moms in my culture. Sorry, Abuelita!)

FAVORITE CANDY: Dark chocolate Kit Kat.

FAVORITE CHILDHOOD BOOK: *El Principito* (*The Little Prince*—in Spanish).

HOW OFTEN I CHECK MY BANK STATEMENT: Two or three times a month max.

A TOOL I ALWAYS WANT TO HAVE IN MY HOUSE: A glue gun or double-sided tape. I'm pretty crafty.

Beatriz's mom was living in San Diego when her contractions began. Beatriz's dad, rather than rush her to the nearest hospital, sped across the border into Tijuana, Mexico. He wanted his baby born there, because he was certain this child would grow up to become president of Mexico. "To be fair, there was no ultrasound, and I'm pretty sure he thought I was a boy!" Beatriz says, laughing.

President of a country may very well be in her future, but for now Beatriz is running a digital media empire called Mitú, cranking out TV shows, videos, and movies aimed at young Latinos. Mitú's shows appear just about everywhere (Facebook, Snapchat, YouTube, Netflix, and more) and have been made with partners you've likely heard of (Paramount, NBC Universo, Spotify, NFL). Every month, 650 million people watch Mitú's content. Michelle Obama was so impressed she invited Beatriz to the White House.

Beatriz was always a go-getter. At age eight, she hatched a crazy plan. "I had a terrible crush on Ricky Martin when he was a kid in this group called Menudo. I needed to meet him so we could fall in love and get married." If she could get a DJ gig at a radio station that played Ricky, she could meet him, and the rest would be history. Well, the fall-in-love part never happened, but she did get hired at the station—while still eight years old—and even got to introduce Menudo once onstage. How did she get the DJ job? She impressed the station owner. An eight-year-old brazen enough to ask for a job? You're hired! She had also done a few decent voice-overs for commercials as a youngster. But most important, she'd argued that she was the demographic the station needed to reach, so she would be much better on-air than some old guy!

Beatriz practiced her deejaying constantly. She'd stand in front of her bedroom mirror announcing the next song and doing fake interviews. By high school, she had her own entertainment segment on a local TV station (which was part of a big Mexican network, Televisa). Her mom would drive her from San Diego to LA to cover the Oscars, and occasionally her interviews would get picked up by the national network. It was the career of her dreams. She saw no reason to go to college, but her mom insisted, so off she went to the University of San Diego. ("To this day, my mom is asking: When am I going to get my master's?") After college, she moved to Mexico City and started working for the country's equivalent of *Entertainment Tonight.* She won three Emmy Awards. She was just twenty-two.

Then a friend gave her life-changing advice: Sell your car, and with the money, make some TV pilots. She listened. She took her first pilot to an industry show in Vegas, where USA Network and Discovery Channel bought her show on the spot. She lied and said, "Of course I have twenty-six segments ready to go!" when really all she had was a short demo. She figured it out along the way, hiring teens to deal with props and art direction so she could focus on the main chaos.

Tip: Sometimes a slight, temporary stretching of the truth is necessary to get your start.

Before long, she made over one thousand hours of content, for companies like Travel Channel, PBS, and MTV. Now she was officially an independent producer. She named her network Mitú. It means "me" and "you" in Spanish. The network launched on YouTube in 2012 and took off. She did make one big mistake. She assumed her viewers spoke Spanish. Nope. Her main viewers consume their content in English. She quickly switched.

Beatriz practiced her deejaying constantly. She'd stand in front of her bedroom mirror announcing the next song and doing fake interviews.

The timing was perfect. Digital TV was just taking off. All the new online platforms needed shows. For $20 million, Beatriz could make a bunch of shows for Facebook and YouTube that would've cost $200 million for premium TV. And she had an advantage over all the other digital frontiersmen chasing the same platforms: She had a target audience she understood, Latino Americans, an ENORMOUS group waiting to be entertained. Until Beatriz came around, no one was writing their life experiences or capturing their particular brand of humor. Whoever won their hearts was going to win big.

To networks and Netflix, Beatriz brought shows like *Chingo Bling: They Can't Deport Us All;* the reality series *Cholos Try, What's Good in Your Hood?, Mom's Movie Review;* and the latest, a comedy sketch called *Brown-town.*

In 2016 she participated in a summit at the White House. Someone asked how she raised $40 million. She answered with three words: White. Man. Swagger. Latino culture emphasizes girls being pretty, quiet, and never aggressive, but Beatriz consciously adopts the overconfident stance most men have naturally. She is outspoken, which helps create an impression of assuredness and competence. But Beatriz still has to work to get her grandma's and mom's voices out of her head telling her to be ladylike.

Tip: Do you have anyone's voice in your head telling you to be ladylike? Who? Think about how this makes you feel. Be strong, smart, bold, good with numbers, and confident—that's ladylike.

More than anything, she loves turning Latino no-name talents into superstars. For years, the movie studios and TV networks had been saying there were too few Latino actresses and actors. False! She would show them. She met Maiah Ocando, a beauty from a teeny Venezuelan town. "I stalked her on YouTube. I was able to get her to the US. I put her in English classes." Now host of *Visto Bueno,* Maiah is very, very big. Beatriz discovered duo Gaby Motomochi and Cris Ordaz making YouTube beauty videos (from their bathroom!) and connected them with the Discovery Channel, where they now host *Gurús de Belleza*

(Beauty Gurus). "Now they're on a billboard in Times Square!" brags Beatriz (as she should).

Someone asked how she raised $40 million. She answered with three words: White. Man. Swagger.

Beatriz swears she isn't a superstar because she has special talent. "If you are truly, truly passionate, and you are willing to put in the work, I promise you'll be successful," she says. Beatriz loves that the internet has created a blank canvas, full of opportunity. Her wisdom for young people: "You don't need to wait to be validated. You can create content and share with an audience. I always say, 'Kids, if you have a phone, you have an opportunity!'"

FITNESS

ELIZABETH CUTLER AND JULIE RICE

COFOUNDERS OF
SOULCYCLE

Business 101: Sweat the details.

THEIR BUSINESS: A beloved chain of eighty-eight (and counting) spin studios offering a guaranteed sweat-fest in their intensive forty-five-minute cardio bike classes. Bonus: Classes are often taught by actors, dancers, and other performers.

ELIZABETH
VERY FIRST JOB: I was a babysitter. I did the dishes. I tidied up.

HIGH SCHOOL GPA: I wasn't the smartest person, but I got good grades.

ON MY BUCKET LIST: I am going to learn to make incredibly delicious food. I want to feed my body, so I want to figure out how to do that.

FAVORITE CANDY: Anything peanut butter and chocolate.

FAVORITE CHILDHOOD BOOK: A biography of Eleanor Roosevelt.

I was obsessed with her service to others and how she met with people when her husband was incapacitated.

ADVICE I'D GIVE TO MY THIRTEEN-YEAR-OLD SELF: Don't worry. (I was worried.) Stay awake. Stay engaged.

JULIE

VERY FIRST JOB: Sneaker store.

HIGH SCHOOL GPA: I got lots of B-minuses and B-pluses [to which Elizabeth interjected, "Hello, she was president of her class!"].

ON MY BUCKET LIST: Visit Greece.

FAVORITE CANDY: A combo of Good & Plenty, dark chocolate nonpareils, and Swedish Fish. I like to mix them all together.

FAVORITE CHILDHOOD BOOK: All Judy Blume books.

ADVICE I'D GIVE TO MY THIRTEEN-YEAR-OLD SELF: All the decisions that seem so big didn't really matter.

This was never the plan, but Julie and Elizabeth started a cult. Do you know what that means? A cult is a group of people with extreme devotion to something or someone—in this case, a regular spin class. Yep, this duo spurred the worship of sweating profusely on a bicycle while packed tight as sardines beside other obsessed, sweaty cyclists. Oh, and crying on the bike. Tears of release, joy, exhaustion, sometimes all at the same time—it's a SoulCycle *thing*.

Julie and Elizabeth's first meeting was the best blind "date" ever—a friend introduced them and they connected as gal pals instantaneously. Both were young moms with five-month-old babies living in New

York City. At one point during that first lunch, their lively conversation jumped to exercise. Julie had recently moved from Los Angeles and was missing how friends there would work out to socialize instead of grabbing drinks. Elizabeth had post-pregnancy weight she wanted to lose, so she was desperate for a form of cardio exercise that motivated her. They talked workouts, and out popped an inspiring idea! How about reimagining spinning, the popular stationary bike workout? Make the classes a fun, feel-good group-bonding experience. Add a spiritual twist. They were both excited enough that they left the res-

> **Tip:** If you leave a lunch or a hangout and an idea has grabbed you so powerfully that you are researching that afternoon, take it as a bright green light. That is your instinct talking.

taurant and immediately began to explore the idea further. That same day. Even that very hour! "We walked out of lunch, and before I had even shut the door of my cab, my cell phone rang, and it was Elizabeth," Julie recalls, "and she said, 'I'm going to look at real estate, and you research towels, and we'll meet on Thursday.'"

Elizabeth eventually found a space on the Upper West Side of Manhattan. New York City real estate is famously pricey, but this rental was weirdly cheap! Why? Well, it was in a former funeral home turned dance studio, and the available room was tucked in back. But it seemed like it could work. So the two decided to go for it and sign a five-year lease. Investing $250,000 of their own money, they bought thirty-three spin bikes, rented towels, and worked with someone to build a basic website. The historic building forbade hanging a sign outside, so they got creative. Elizabeth bought a little cart called a rickshaw, which people ride around in on the streets of India; painted it bright yellow; and parked it out front as their "sign." Unfortunately, they routinely got sixty-five-dollar fines from the building management, but they reasoned it was just a cost of doing business.

"We walked out of lunch, and before I had even shut the door of my cab, my cell phone rang, and it was Elizabeth," Julie recalls, "and she said, 'I'm going to look at real estate, and you research towels, and we'll meet on Thursday.'"

Next, they brainstormed what their dream spin class would feel like. They pictured a dimly lit room, because darkness made them feel less inhibited about their bodies and movements. Candles would create a soothing atmosphere. Julie had been a Hollywood agent, so if she knew one thing, it was how to spot talent. She pictured the instructor as a performer. Teachers would be actors, dancers, and hip-hop artists. "We've always thought of it [each class] as a mini production. Curtain up, curtain down," says Julie.

> **Tip:** Learn how to hear no as an invitation to continue forward with a slight work-around.

The duo was continually asking themselves, *How else should Soul-Cycle feel different?* "We put a lot of emphasis on what it would feel like coming through the door." It wasn't just the time on the bike. So they considered every tiny detail of the *full* experience. Julie always forgets socks for the gym, so how about having spare pairs available? Same with hair ties. To counteract the sweat, the smell should be fresh and citrusy. They found the perfect grapefruit-scented candles for the reception area. The studio look should be cheery rather than black and metallic like most urban gyms. They picked sunny yellow as their color. They also treated customers like friends. Like they mattered. "If you preferred room temperature water instead of cold, we remembered that," says Julie. "We always thought we were in the hospitality business more than the fitness business."

Once they opened their first spin studio, they needed to attract customers. One trick they tried was printing up two hundred T-shirts and getting them into the hands of cool New Yorkers they or their friends knew. Visibility was key: Someone was bound to see the shirts and ask, "What's SoulCycle?" Hoping for media coverage, they turned boring press kits into goody bags, so that the informational paperwork was bundled with a T-shirt and a class pass. They pictured themselves popping in on health and beauty editors in their offices and chatting them up as they handed over the bag. Instead, they never got anywhere near the twenty-seventh floor or the eighteenth floor, where the desired editors sat. They were always stopped in the lobby by security and told to just drop the bag there. That idea was a bust. But luckily, the T-shirt giveaways and word of mouth drummed up just enough riders for classes to not be embarrassingly empty.

Their next marketing concept was a home run: a pop-up studio in the Hamptons, where fancy New Yorkers—with thirty dollars to drop on a bike class—escaped for the summer. If people fell for SoulCycle on a beach vacation, they would look for it back in the city. Summer ended and—jackpot—soon, three hundred to four hundred people were perspiring all over their city studio floor every day! Next, they were opening new studios around New York, then California, then DC and Boston. And they just keep on spinning.

Julie and Elizabeth discovered quickly that they have complementary skills. Elizabeth is good at finance, technology, and studio design. She came from the real estate industry. (Her mom got her real estate license at age forty and became a top seller in their Chicago suburb. She's Elizabeth's hero, and Elizabeth followed her into real estate.) Julie, meanwhile, is a people person. Her talent-scouting background prepared her for all hiring, training, and marketing required. "Together we're kind of one perfect CEO," said Julie. At that first lunch, they obviously didn't know what a perfect partnership they were. But they had a feeling. "I think our partnership is kind of the biggest part of our story," says Julie. "There are very few sets of female partners out there that have been able to stay together."

> **Tip:** Assess your own skill set. What are you best at? Now find people to work with you, whether a partner or coworkers, who excel at doing the things you stink at.

Remaining harmonious as cofounders hasn't been effortless. When their communication got a little dicey, they quickly hired a coach to help them. One important skill the coach taught was active listening. This means putting some structure around talking and listening so you really pay attention and hear what the other person is saying. An exercise they learned was where one person talks for five minutes while the other just listens. They also tried sitting with their thoughts for a day before reacting. "We would then make time to sit together and problem-solve," Elizabeth recounts.

It was these skills that helped them weather a reservation system melt-down that hit after six straight years of growth. SoulCyclists book their classes for the week beginning on Mondays at noon, down to the exact bike, and by 2012, log-in numbers at that hour had ratcheted up to fifty thousand frenzied cycle fanatics. The platform to handle this barrage had been designed when the company was much smaller. But when Soul-Cycle upgraded, the new system started off with some major kinks. Imagine how annoyed riders were to show up and find seven others scheduled for the same bike. Seven! It was bad. Really bad. They ended up having to take reservations manually, "turning our office effectively into a call center," Elizabeth remembers. It took a while to pinpoint the problem, and they were out of their knowledge zone. Their takeaway: "All girls should learn how to code. At least know enough to hire the right people and to then understand what they are telling you," Elizabeth adds.

"I think our partnership is kind of the biggest part of our story," says Julie. "There are very few sets of female partners out there that have been able to stay together."

Between the two women, they have four daughters, ages seven to six-teen. A key benefit of being entrepreneurs is no matter how hard they work, they still dictate their daily schedules. They can make time to go on a school field trip or take a daughter for her flu shot. Still, CEO life is chaotic. Out of need, they often weave their daughters into their Soul-Cycle work. Their girls have worked the desk. They've traveled to help open studios in new cities. A true victory for Elizabeth was hearing her daughter recount the time a boy told her that only guys are CEOs. She whipped back, "Uh-uh! My mom is a CEO."

HOME

SUZY BATIZ

FOUNDER AND CEO OF
POO-POURRI

Business 101: Humor sells.

HER BUSINESS: Sprays and potions that turn life's stinks (human and cat poo, sweat-stanky shoes) into fresh, happy scents. And the latest addition: home cleaning products.

VERY FIRST JOB: Burger King, but I didn't get to work the window, because I "wasn't cute enough" [in the words of her twenty-year-old male manager. . . . Whatever!].

AS A KID, WHAT I WANTED TO BE WHEN I GREW UP: Fashion designer, but I didn't even know that was a job.

A WEIRD THING YOU'LL FIND ON (OR IN) MY DESK: Incense and palo santo sticks (removes negative energy) and tarot cards or runes.

HIGH SCHOOL GPA: C–minus at best (total grading on a curve).

MY BEDTIME: Nine-thirty p.m. (I wake up at five-thirty a.m.)

ON MY BUCKET LIST: Visiting Bhutan.

A GUILTY PLEASURE: Mexican food, which I rarely eat.

FAVORITE CANDY: Salted caramel.

FAVORITE CHILDHOOD BOOK: Nancy Drew mysteries.

AN EXPRESSION I USE A LOT THAT PEOPLE KNOW ME FOR: "Anything is possible—find a way!"

HOW OFTEN I CHECK MY BANK STATEMENT: Um, never. I haven't balanced my checkbook since I was nineteen years old.

A TOOL I ALWAYS WANT TO HAVE IN MY HOUSE: A thirty-foot-long duster. I have a cobweb now that's in one of the peaks of my house and it's driving me crazy. If you have a duster, please send it over.

ADVICE I'D GIVE TO MY THIRTEEN-YEAR-OLD SELF: Nothing is ever as bad as it seems right now; it will all change. It always does.

Suzy is like a phoenix that rises from the ashes. Only in this story, Suzy rises up from a pile of POOP. She will proudly tell you that poop is her specialty.

The product that has made her millions and millions is called Poo-Pourri. It comes in a little bottle that you spritz into the toilet bowl before doing your business. And voilà, the whole darn potty emits scents of citrus or lavender vanilla or eucalyptus. It is honestly quite miraculous, the job this tiny bottle performs.

Suzy grew up poor in a small Arkansas town. The only doll clothes she had she sewed herself. Nobody was thinking about paying for pretty smells. "It's surely the reason I'm a natural maker," she says. She had gaps in her smile from baby teeth that never grew in, and as she tells it, she *really* needed braces! But the family could never afford them. She only got her "train tracks" at age seventeen, paid for by

a greasy burger-flipping job at Burger King. School, meanwhile, always beat her down. There was no nurturing of creative types; and her people smarts didn't help her on pop algebra quizzes or get her through her English papers. School just didn't make her feel smart. She quit college because her sixty-hours-a-week job as the youngest manager of an apparel superstore was impossible to balance with her coursework.

Looking for a creative outlet, she launched a handful of entrepreneurial ventures, all of them failures. A tanning salon. A bridal salon (she painted the windows black to make the white gowns pop—bomb!). Unable to make these businesses go, she filed for bankruptcy, twice. The bank took her car to cover her unpaid bills.

She quit college because her sixty-hours-a-week job as the youngest manager of an apparel superstore was impossible to balance with her coursework.

One night after she "swore off all business," Suzy was eating dinner with some friends and family. The topic (somehow) turned to bathroom stink, and her brother-in-law, who knew Suzy was a wiz with scents and essential oils, wondered aloud whether odors could be trapped so they couldn't sour the air. What happened then in Suzy's brain felt like a spray of shooting stars. She has named the feeling "Radical

Resonance." It's an instance of your universe suddenly aligning in a completely cosmic way, she says. You know it's happening because you get goose bumps. You feel high on caffeine yet haven't consumed even a sip of Diet Coke. And the idea clings to you like an obsessive middle school crush.

You see, Suzy, the aromatherapy ace, knew the answer to her brother-in-law's question. Yes, oils did "trap" other smells. And, Suzy thought to herself, a few drops of the right mix of oils in the toilet could potentially trap and neutralize *those* horrible smells. The revelation was HUGE!

And, put to the test, it worked. Suzy played around with oil mixtures for a year, and finally found a revolutionary formula. A few sprays into the bowl before going, and a film formed on the surface that held all the bad smells under the water. Think of all the embarrassment she could save everyone.

Next, to spread word of her invention, she decided to produce a promo video. She convinced a renowned creative team that had made other viral videos to work with her. The writers and videographers and Suzy spent days in a mountain cabin in Utah brainstorming ideas. What they came out with was a hysterically funny two-minute spot called "Girls Don't Poop." The video's story line was so outrageous that Suzy could find only four actresses who would even audition. The chosen actress had to speak her lines from a seated position on the toilet. It was a potty-humor masterpiece. After the video went wild (40,921,176 You-Tube views), Poo-Pourri sales increased by 90 percent. A viral home-run like that is as unlikely as the (very rare) white rhino. The spray sells everywhere from Target to Ulta Beauty to Urban Outfitters.

It was a potty-humor masterpiece.

Suzy leads by intuition. She considers this a feminine form of leader-ship and believes it rare and distinct from the common male approach of straight-up number crunching and strategy. She says her best deci-sions are based on gut feelings, and a sense of "flow." Right now, she's feeling positive about a new partnership with Gwyneth Paltrow and her Goop brand, to launch Poo-Pourri's all-natural-ingredients home-cleaning product line, Supernatural, in 2018. The witty marketing phrase: "Clean Butt Naked."

> **Tip:** Take your orders from your gut instincts. When you feel like a rainbow just parked overhead, charge forward. When you feel like a nest of yellow jackets just bombarded your bedroom, stop and reconsider.

She's feeling a lot less flow when it comes to a line of cat litter spray. Her team had been nose-to-the-ground on the product for over a year, but the oils for the litter continue to clump. Then a cat around the office got sick, and product testers weren't sure why. Frus-trated, the team froze the project. Suzy didn't care how much time they had already devoted. Only winning products in her line!

"A lot of people come to me with good ideas but not many with a great idea. When you have your idea, nurture it until it's amazing . . . so good that people can't wait to tell other people about it," she says.

Suzy's intuition and flow have her rethinking her first viral video, too, the one that made her famous . . . or infamous. Looking back, she's now appalled that she further perpetuated the ridiculous belief that "girls don't poop," insinuating that it's unladylike or shameful. It was "the wrong message entirely," she says now. She's released a new video called "Girls Do Poop." Some lines from the new script: "Let's start a movement, a bowel movement . . ." and "The powers are yours alone, to sit down and own your throne."

Funny really does sell.

TINA SHARKEY

COFOUNDER AND CEO OF
BRANDLESS

Business 101: Don't just invent a product or launch a business. Start a movement.

HER BUSINESS: A line of "brandless" home, personal care, and food products made as healthfully, ecologically, and ethically as possible. Get your fluoride-free toothpaste and non-GMO organic agave nectar here. Oh, and almost everything costs three dollars.

A WEIRD THING YOU'LL FIND ON (OR IN) MY DESK: A cucumber spray that I love the scent of—eau de whatever. It's very fresh. I'm bummed, though, because the company went out of business.

HIGH SCHOOL GPA: [Eye roll] I don't remember.

WORST SUBJECT IN SCHOOL: Physics.

VERY FIRST JOB: I was a model at Bloomingdale's as a young teen. In fourth grade, I'd make gourmet desserts for my mom's friends' parties. I loved using the pastry bag. I'd make meringues shaped like mushrooms.

AS A KID, WHAT I WANTED TO BE WHEN I GREW UP: An entrepreneur.

MY BEDTIME: Eleven p.m.

ON MY BUCKET LIST: I always wanted to go to Japan for cherry blossom season, and I wanted to go to the NBA All-Star Weekend. I just did both.

A GUILTY PLEASURE: Long hot showers. I feel bad about wasting water, but it's hard to get out.

FAVORITE CANDY: I'm not a big candy person.

FAVORITE CHILDHOOD BOOK: *Alice in Wonderland.*

HOW OFTEN I CHECK MY BANK STATEMENT: I check the sales numbers every single day, probably two or three times. We meet to look at our numbers once a week. If anything is off, I know about it right away.

ADVICE I'D GIVE TO MY THIRTEEN-YEAR-OLD SELF: If you don't believe in yourself, no one's going to believe in you.

Tina Sharkey knows how to keep a secret. In the first eighteen months of Brandless, she quietly filed a trademark on the name. She trademarked the Brandless look—simple, single-color packaging. To keep things extra hush-hush, she and her cofounder, Ido Leffler, a lifelong friend, created a fake company name: Dosey. They made fake Dosey business cards, a fake Dosey website, and even a fake Dosey Instagram profile! They wanted to avoid tipping off the giant product companies, like Procter & Gamble, who they were about to take on as competitors.

In fact, all potential partners and employees they met were required to sign NDAs (nondisclosure agreements). NDAs are like a business version of "cross my heart and hope to die, stick a needle in my eye." It is a legal document that binds you to not reveal anything that is shared, allowing business talk to happen but secrets to stay secret.

So what exactly is Brandless, this idea they were so desperate to keep TOP-SECRET? Brandless provides a curated selection of the basic things you use every day. These include things like toilet paper, lotion, cooking spoons, and crunchy popcorn snacks, to name a few. Brandless aims to provide the healthiest, most cruelty-free and chemical-free, ethically sound, good-for-the-planet choices. It also provides them at a lower cost than name-brand products. Who doesn't love a good bargain, right?

Tina and Ido are making goods both better and cheaper by taking on overadvertised, overpackaged, and overpriced consumer goods. Instead of buying name brands, like Lay's potato chips or Tampax tampons, they want you to purchase their brandless basics, which won't be using the age-old practices that add cost and reduce quality (more on that later). They are driven by a strong philosophy: customers are being fleeced and deserve better. They see Brandless as a movement rather than a company—"a movement of people who reject labels, legacy institutions, and old ways of doing things," Tina says.

Brandless began in a brainstorming session. Tina and Ido were hunting for a business idea, so they smartly started by riffing on the things in society that really need fixing. They landed on massive consumer goods companies—

like Procter & Gamble, Unilever, and General Mills—that own the market.

You may be thinking, *How can Brandless set such low prices?* The main explanation is in their name: brand*less*. Known brands like Oreo cookies or Crest toothpaste cost more because the companies behind them know customers will pay up for the recognizable name. It's a vicious cycle, because to stay top-of-mind, they must advertise constantly, which is very costly. That boosts the price even more.

> *Tina sees Brandless as a movement rather than a company—"a movement of people who reject labels, legacy institutions, and old ways of doing things."*

Not only does Brandless not pay for slick ads and fancy packaging, they actually squeeze cost out of manufacturing and distribution by doing it all themselves. They are also online only, so they bypass stores, which means no paying the likes of Rite Aid or Safeway the shelving fees that big stores charge for prime placement. Brandless calls all the annoying marketing, retailer, and shelving costs they are avoiding "Brand Tax," and Tina successfully trademarked the term because it so perfectly describes what she is fighting with Brandless.

Brandless quotes that their products are on average 40 percent cheaper than everyone else's, but their bigger goal is to produce products that are safe for the body and the earth. Many of their foods are organic and gluten-free. Many of their cosmetics are sulfate-free and paraben-free. They don't use synthetic dyes. A product search feature on Brandless.com is "cruelty-free." (Now, that's novel!) They even offer a "tree-free" category: toilet paper, napkins, and tissues made from sugarcane and bamboo grass.

To launch Brandless, Tina cooked up a clever PR trick. Her team posted on Craigslist calling for actors for a food-tasting gig. Why actors? They wanted extra-expressive types, because Tina was utterly certain tasters would go gaga for her snacks, and she wanted to capture some extreme enthusiasm. Twelve actors came to their offices for a food fest—sweet potato chips, dill pickle popcorn, pasta sauce. After thirty minutes, they were led into Brandless's "lab," a room filled with shelves lined with products arranged by color, and asked, "What would you think if we told you every single delicious item here costs three dollars?" They gasped (happy gasps), hooted, and went bug-eyed in amazement, all while being filmed by Tina and crew. The scene became the Brandless launch ad. They called the clip "Awesome Strangers" (you can watch it on YouTube).

Stunts that grab attention are clearly Tina's sweet spot. She snagged Steph Curry as an investor and cheerleader, winning him over with an inspired speech about building "for profit and for purpose." In the speech, she talked about acts of kindness and a world where service workers are all in the game. Halfway through, Steph interrupted and said, "Mic drop, Sharkey. We're getting behind you. I want to invest." (She cried.) More celebrities followed, including Ariana Grande and her agent, Scooter Braun, and bareMinerals founder Leslie Blodgett (page 121).

A slogan Tina uses is "Democratizing goodness." The idea behind it is that stuff that's good for you shouldn't just be for the super lucky who can shop at Whole Foods (sometimes derisively called "Whole Paycheck"). She believes all people deserve better—better stuff, better food, a better life. "Everyone deserves it, and it's not okay to have a divide [of haves and have-nots]." She says she's trying to live in a "United States of Goodness." To that end, for every order, Brandless donates one meal to a hungry family through the nonprofit Feeding America.

When Tina was younger, it seemed she was destined to work in fashion. Her grandfather and father worked in the garment industry. Her mom became president of big-time fashion brand Perry Ellis, and Tina frequently did homework at the company conference table.

Tina believes all people deserve better—
better stuff, better food, a better life.

But that wasn't her passion. She liked and still likes building communities. At the start of her career, she cofounded iVillage, which became the largest online destination for women in the early days of the internet. She then ran BabyCenter, another massive online community, this one for moms and moms-to-be. (In 2009, 50 percent of the babies born in the United States were registered on BabyCenter, and 80 percent of new and expectant moms visited the site. Clearly, this idea rocked.)

For a year after she struck on the Brandless idea, she kept her day job, funding and advising start-ups. When her idea slipped out to a venture capitalist friend, however, she knew something had to give. The moneyman said he'd love to "seed" her, meaning invest a small amount of money and help her grow her seedling idea into something Jack-and-the-beanstalk big. Soon, that investor plus a bunch of new ones plunked $16 million in her bank account; it became Brandless's series-A funding.

> **Tip:** Venture capital funding happens in stages, referred to as series A, B, C, etc. Series A is the first money a company raises from VC firms. Series C means it's the third time the company has gone out and raised new investment money to grow the business. And so on.

Then, in 2017, nearing launch and wanting to grow faster, Tina fundraised again. In 2018, VC firm SoftBank boosted Brandless by investing a monumental $240 million in a series-C round. Based on that amount, the media reported that Tina must be taking on Amazon. About sixty hours after opening their "doors," someone on Tina's team texted her *48*. Forty-eight orders? No. Orders had come in from ALL forty-eight states (they can't yet ship to Alaska or Hawaii).

PACKAGING

JESSE GENET

COFOUNDER AND CEO OF
LUMI

Business 101: The best ideas impact large numbers of people.

HER BUSINESS: She makes boxes and all things packaging, handling shipping for the new generation of web retailers.

VERY FIRST JOB: I was nineteen. I was really struggling for money to survive, so I took a paid internship at a Korean fashion company in Los Angeles. It was almost like a sweatshop.

A WEIRD THING YOU'LL FIND ON (OR IN) MY DESK: Dog treats, a glass fish, a tiny Airstream trailer. People give me very weird things.

WORST SUBJECT IN SCHOOL: Maybe history, but only because I had a bad teacher. I love history; I just really didn't like the memorization.

MY BEDTIME: Eleven or midnight.

ON MY BUCKET LIST: I want to build a house.

A GUILTY PLEASURE: I choose to drive classic cars (1972 Chevy truck currently), so they are never working well.

FAVORITE CANDY: Gummy vitamins (way too many of them).

FAVORITE CHILDHOOD BOOK: *A Separate Peace.*

HOW OFTEN I CHECK MY SALES: I refresh the data every forty-five seconds. We have a way to see the orders coming in.

AN EXPRESSION I USE A LOT THAT PEOPLE KNOW ME FOR: "Geez oh Peets oh geez." (It's a Michigan expression.)

Jesse's company, Lumi, began with a wild-goose chase to hunt down a weird dye. At sixteen, she was passed over for cross-country team captain, and she felt like her life was ruined and she just needed to *do* something that made her feel worthwhile. This led her to launch a T-shirt biz. She shot lots of arty photos to print onto shirts with colorful dye.

With a headful of design ambitions, she burrowed into learning about the printing process, and the actual chemistry of how solvents interact with each other and with light to produce different effects. The basement of her Detroit suburb home quickly filled with smelly (and toxic!) solutions and odd screen presses. She used every birthday and Christmas gift request to acquire this stuff. But despite tinkering endlessly, she couldn't get her photos to achieve the original look she was after—wrapping around the arm or up the side seam. She sought advice at a local screen-printing shop, but the guys there said her concept was impossible.

She continued digging for alternative techniques, but meanwhile created a bunch of shirts using just standard screen printing. What to do with a fresh pile of shirts? She was sixteen, and she begged her parents to let her spend her summer in LA, living with a family friend and selling her shirts.

They went for the outlandish plan, she believes, because she put together a very comprehensive (and charming) proposal about why Los Angeles was the ultimate place for T-shirt selling, and going there was essential to growing her business. "I made a chart of all the boutiques in LA, and how many more were there compared to Detroit. They were impressed with all the homework I did," she says. They said okay. Though she didn't tell them this directly, she was desperate for more independence. "I always wanted to get as far away from my parents as possible."

> **Tip:** Write down five things that make you really anxious. Speaking in front of the class? Timed mile in gym? Talking to someone you like (as in *like* like)? Now find a way to do the scary thing several times. The scary factor decreases with experience.

In LA, she cruised hip Melrose Avenue, pacing in front of boutiques until she got up the nerve to go inside and ask them to stock her tees. She was truly winging it. "It was me with a clipboard of order forms and some little business cards and my shirts. All I knew about how this might happen was from watching TV," she says. She got in touch with her inner moxie and convinced some stores to sell her shirts. Her takeaway: Withstand the butterflies—they eventually subside. "Today's nerve-racking thing is tomorrow's normal thing."

Fast-forward two years. Jesse was still obsessing over flexible printing methods that would lead to supremely unique designs. She was back in Los Angeles, having graduated high school after junior year (she had read an obscure policy stating that you just needed a few signatures to graduate early, begged her mom and dad, and voilà, freedom). She scrapped her University of Michigan plan to pursue art school. She needed a portfolio, so she watched YouTube videos on how to create the pieces the ArtCenter College of Design would need to see. Meanwhile, she kept unearthing obscure printing techniques, deciphering the process behind photo development, hoping to figure out how to transfer photos the way she wanted. In one musty book, she spotted a reference to a 1950s chemical, a light-activated fabric dye invented by an outfit called the Gibson Paint Company, which sounded weirdly promising. More sleuthing revealed that the inventor was dead and Gibson was gone, but a new company was selling the product. A lead, but then, *pop*—her bubble burst—that company was also closed down.

In LA, she cruised hip Melrose Avenue, pacing in front of boutiques until she got up the nerve to go inside and ask them to stock her tees. She was truly winging it.

But the owner was still alive, and she nipped at him like a desperate puppy, writing multiple letters (snail mail; he had no email) asking questions about his dye. He didn't reply. So she called him. He didn't answer. Ultimately, she drove six hours to Walnut Creek, California, and knocked on his door. He opened it, and she asked if he'd share or sell the formula. He resisted. She negotiated hard, racking her brain for how to convince him. "It was like *The Art of the Deal.* I had to figure out what would motivate him," she says. She determined that he mostly cared about selling off his garage full of dust-gathering leftover dye. She offered to buy it and load it into a U-Haul, in exchange for his trade secrets, like how to formulate it. He agreed.

Art school started, and instantly she was overwhelmed. She had become intrigued with art and design so late in high school that she had almost no formal training. Despite getting accepted to Art-Center thanks to those YouTube videos, she felt ill-prepared relative to her classmates. "I had no business being there," she says. Luckily, she befriended Stephan, an amazing talent who helped her survive. Now he's Lumi's cofounder. She raved to him about Inkodye, and he said, "COOL! Let's launch the product broadly!" And they did.

The pair did a Kickstarter campaign and raised $13K. (It was just after Kickstarter had launched, so first Jesse and Stephan had to explain what Kickstarter even was!) Soon the Lumi duo did a second

> **Tip:** If you are excited enough to get someone else fully excited, that should tell you something. Do that idea!

Kickstarter, raising $269K. It was enough for them to start producing DIY art kits. Eventually those were selling in Urban Outfitters and Michaels. Sports brand Puma partnered with Lumi to make Inkodyed shoes. Jesse and Stephan even created printed furniture that sold at renowned ABC Carpet & Home in New York. In 2014, Lumi was profitable, selling $1.2 million worth of dye. Jesse even won a prize for Best Art Supply of the year. "The other winner was a pipe cleaner company. What's more freaking random than winning *that* prize?" she says, laughing. Such kudos felt bizarre because making her name in crafting kits was definitely not something Jesse ever expected!

But soon, selling just one item got boring. Jesse and Stephan applied to and got a slot at the Y Combinator (YC) start-up incubator, which is like winning the lottery. It's truly harder to get into than Harvard! Incubators generally are wildly popular, basically mini boot camps for entrepreneurs that teach founders much of what they need to turn their idea into a real company. You get accepted by giving a knockout pitch, a snappy, persuasive presentation of the idea. The YC incubator has deep connections in Silicon Valley and was the birthplace of monster successes like Airbnb, Reddit, and Dropbox. Tracy Young's PlanGrid (page 255) also has the YC seal of approval.

The YC philosophy is distinct and pushed their thinking. In a nutshell: Why shoot small? What BIG idea would exploit so much printing knowledge? "They [Y Combinator] really inspire a certain type of thinking. They ask, How many people or companies are you going to impact with your business? They emphasize *reach.* They say, Okay, you could make the best scheduling app for trapeze artists ever, but if you are so good at that, why can't your app be applicable to every hourly performer?" she says.

In 2015, Lumi was reborn as a packaging company (Lumi 2.0, in Silicon Valley speak). Businesses come for everything they need to box up and ship their products. Don't be thinking, *Yaaaawn.* Lumi and Jesse are so NOT boring! "We were building the product we wished we'd had when launching Inkodye," she says. That is, a newbie entrepreneur could take a business that opened on a Friday with one product and some marketing photos and figure out how to get that product wrapped up, boxed, and shipped.

The shift in company focus—or **pivot,** in start-up lingo—makes sense. Tons of start-ups pivot toward what the world needs and what they do best. Packaging requires custom printing, to personalize the boxes and make cool stickers for the tissue paper and to make branded labels so everything's matchy-matchy. And Jesse knows custom printing. "The fascination with dye chemistry, ink chemistry, printing processes is what makes us very good at custom packaging, because whether a box looks fantastic or not comes down to the printing," she said. The idea for a company rarely comes fully formed in a flash of brilliance. "People think of entrepreneurs as all having this lightning-bolt idea. But those stories are written in reverse, once they know what they have become."

A key Lumi client is MeUndies, an LA underwear company that makes briefs with skulls, jellyfish, and even avocados on them. Certainly, their mailer has to be colorful and standout, not just standard brown. That's where Lumi shines. Jesse understands that in this era of mail-order everything, the box is important branding. Lumi also packages up the monthly subscription box of trendy kids' clothes for Rockets of Awesome and skin care by Supergoop! They even pack Burrow sofas. Imagine boxing up a four-seater king sofa to transport to Tennessee or North Dakota! A cool thing Lumi does is geo-locate the best box manufacturers as close as possible to where products are made or warehoused, saving companies money by not having their boxes flying around before there's even anything in them.

"People think of entrepreneurs as all having this lightning-bolt idea. But those stories are written in reverse, once they know what they have become."

Jesse lives in a chrome vintage Airstream trailer. She parks it behind Lumi in Los Angeles. "I have refined what I need to a monk-like level.

I really enjoy not needing a lot, kind of an exercise in 'What do you really need to feel at home?'" she says. She hosts a silly podcast called *Shipping Things.* Working ambitiously yet not taking herself too seriously is a goal. "We're shipping boxes, not handling the nuclear codes."

CONSTRUCTION

TRACY YOUNG

COFOUNDER AND CEO OF
PLANGRID

Business 101: If your idea makes an industry/ job/anything faster, more convenient, cheaper— you've hit gold.

HER BUSINESS: Digitizing the giant, hard-to-carry sets of architectural plans used by builders on construction projects.

A WEIRD THING YOU'LL FIND ON (OR IN) MY DESK: Maybe a new-born baby (born in 2018!).

HIGH SCHOOL GPA: 3.3—just good enough to get into college.

WORST SUBJECT IN SCHOOL: Probably PE. I was usually skipping to be in the art studio.

VERY FIRST JOB: Mermaid Aquarium in Fremont, California. Cleaning tanks and staring at fishies.

ON MY BUCKET LIST: Seeing the northern lights. Being category king (or queen) for the construction software industry.

A GUILTY PLEASURE: Chocolate cake.

Tracy gets inspiration from a weird source: cute animal videos. She watches them constantly, which is how beavers and honey badgers became her role models. Beavers work hard and are patient. They build dams piece by piece, just like she built PlanGrid piece by piece. ("If you find a shortcut to this, please email me at tracy@plangrid.com," she has told audiences.) Honey badgers fight lions and eat poisonous snakes to survive. In a similar (but less violent) way, Tracy is disrupting the conventional old construction industry, forcing modernization by putting building plans and tools for construction work online.

Yes, before YouTube videos and iPads, things were done mostly on paper. People wrote letters instead of emails. They sent invitations, not Evites. They paid with a crisp twenty-dollar bill instead of via PayPal or Venmo or Apple Pay. And construction workers followed detailed room-by-room plans on paper sheets called blueprints. So Tracy had to teach traditionalists new tricks. Luckily, back before PlanGrid, she'd had some practice challenging convention.

At California State University, she studied civil engineering, a male-dominated field. Right after, she went to work as a project engineer building hospitals, also something girls don't often do (just 9 percent of the construction industry is female). The all-guys crew did much of their important decision-making clumped together taking cigarette breaks. Tracy was so desperate to participate fully that she temporarily took up the grossest and unhealthiest habit of all—smoking. (She quickly canned the tactic—nothing was worth that.) It was while triple-checking that nine hundred hospital rooms were being built to specifications, carrying around such a load of oversized blueprints that she needed a special cart, when she said there MUST be a better way.

The idea was really obvious: find a technology to digitize those thick stacks of full newspaper spread–sized blue-and-white line drawings, usually curled into fat rolls, that builders are constantly struggling to lug, unfurl, and keep up to date. If computerized, changes could be zapped straight to workers' iPads. Apple's first iPad had just come out, which is a key piece of PlanGrid's success story. PlanGrid piggybacked that technical advance. Digital plans are also much cheaper. A bound paper set of plans for a sprawling office building or new airport terminal detailing every toilet and electrical outlet can cost $23,000, or even more, and often multiple sets are needed to reflect changes. Major construction companies can spend an insane $4 billion on blueprints annually.

Tip: Build off cultural trends and technological leaps. They provide a wide-open door for new businesses. Think about the e-scooter invasion in many cities. Someone is going to invent the hip scooter helmet or the well-configured urban scooter commuter bag. Opportunity awaits!

Tracy teamed up with her construction engineer pal from college, Ryan, to attempt to make her vision real. But the obstacle they faced is common among start-ups. "It's the saddest story in Silicon Valley," says Tracy. "Two domain experts [meaning they were construction experts; that's their domain] with no technical expertise." Many ideas rely on technology, but not all good idea people are technically inclined. So they did what ambitious non–STEM-savvy entrepreneurs must do: find techies. They quickly hired an engineer and three software developers as cofounders.

The gang of founders knew that start-ups require round-the-clock work, so they decided to move in together. They rented a house in Sunnyvale, California. They worked until one a.m. every night around the coffee table (trying hopelessly to keep the white carpet clean) and resumed at seven a.m. They took turns cooking, oftentimes rice and beans (Tracy is vegan). Their home/work pad felt made for TV. "It was very much like *The Social Network* [a movie about Mark Zuckerberg founding Facebook], minus the pool parties," Tracy told *USA Today.*

Just 9 percent of the construction industry is female.

After the team created the software to put building plans online, they needed builders to test it. They bought a dozen iPads, all maxing out their credit cards to the $5,000 limit. "If the whole venture flopped, our backup was selling them off on eBay," Tracy says. Luckily that wasn't necessary. Tracy and team loaded their software onto the iPads and gave the tablets to local builders. Initially, the construction folks were skeptical. The iPad was so fragile. Wouldn't it smash to pieces in five minutes? Within three months, though, all but one tester wanted to pay to continue using PlanGrid. Today, PlanGrid boasts over 1 million projects, in 80 countries, including blueprints for the Facebook campus and Target, Chick-fil-A, and Victoria's Secret stores. Tracy tweeted out some gushing compliments from customers: "I felt like I was using fire for the first time." "Greatest invention since the cordless drill."

The PlanGrid founding team experienced a very personal tragedy early on. One of the developers in their group, Antoine, passed away from cancer. Today, Tracy still uses this massive loss to keep perspective for the company. Relative to cancer, nothing is hard. She can push through any obstacle.

About a year into the company's life, in 2012, PlanGrid's founders were standout enough to get invited into the über-selective Y Combinator (YC) incubator. Tracy took charge to assure their pitch was knockout. She had the team do a dry run of their interview fifty to one hundred times to make sure the presentation ran smoothly. It did the trick.

At the YC three-month program's end, the incubator teams pitch again, this time to real investors, for real money. Tracy and team raised their first $1.5 million there (including from YC's president—a serious confidence boost). Later they raised $55 million more. Big checks like that allowed the company to run fast, which they wanted to do because their customers were pushing for more. They wanted PlanGrid to digitize change orders, field notes, and inspection reports, and to enable scribbling notes in the digital blueprint margins.

Tracy has a nose for picking up every tidbit of knowledge sprinkled in her path. She finds her way like Hansel and Gretel, heeding the crumbs. At YC, for instance, some wise entrepreneurs suggested firing workers who needed firing, and doing it fast. Why? Because sometimes employees just aren't a fit for your company, or they don't have quite the experience they said they did, and that's often revealed quickly. Once you know this, don't delay, because the mess they inevitably make just expands like grape juice spilled on a white bedspread. Putting away ego also helps her pick up tips from others. "I always ask for help. I always tell my team when I don't understand what they are talking about," she says.

Sometimes, though, the rookie CEO just has to learn the hard way—by flubbing. Tracy's idea to abolish all job titles and seniority levels was a disaster. It made decision-making harder and confused everyone. Her office space planning was a fail, too. Within months, she figured out that she should have bought smaller desks. Not long after they moved in, PlanGrid was already outgrowing its office space.

As a first-time CEO, she has come to accept that problems are an everyday reality. One trick is chopping big ones into bite-sized chunks. When the company was barely attracting any female employees, a large and complex problem, she tried small initiatives like tweaking the language in their online job postings. Using the word *ninjas* to describe the nimble, fierce coders and engineers they wanted to hire was clever but, she discovered, unintentionally signaled "male." By simply rewording their employment ads, she boosted female applicants meaningfully.

> **Tip:** Tasks that seem terrifying start to feel doable when you break them down. So, ten-page history paper due next Friday? Okay, don't hide under the covers binge-watching bad baking shows and moaning you might barf and faint simultaneously. Try this instead: Tonight, brainstorm paper topics. Tomorrow, research your favorite three, and pick one. On day three, gather research materials. Day four, write an outline. Better, right?

PlanGrid is obsessed with customer service. The company's average response time to inquiries is just a few hours. A box on PlanGrid's home page provides a live chat twelve hours a day. Every employee is required to work in customer service for a period (which includes being the live chatter). Tracy listens and responds to complaints, and insists others do the same, because she truly cares about making construction sites run more efficiently. Interviewed by *USA Today,* Tracy commented, "When you're building a start-up, a company, you have to find a problem that is worth years—actually, decades—of your life." PlanGrid is her calling.

So much of Tracy's fire comes from her parents. They escaped the Vietnam War, were picked up by the Malaysia Coast Guard and taken to a refugee camp in Laos, and eventually got to the United States with nothing. Her whole childhood they struggled. "Whatever the line was for homelessness, we were just above. We were always in poverty," she says. But they persevered, working multiple jobs each, and eventually started a restaurant **wholesale** food business. They put two kids through college. "It's easy for me to work hard. I want to honor them," Tracy says.

So much of Tracy's fire comes from her parents. They escaped the Vietnam War, were picked up by the Malaysia Coast Guard and taken to a refugee camp in Laos, and eventually got to the United States with nothing.

The latest PlanGrid development is beyond honorable. Tracy made a product so compelling, so red-hot amazing, the venerable architecture and design software developer Autodesk just *had* to have it for their very own. At the close of 2018, Autodesk paid $874 million for Plan-Grid. Entrepreneurs normally only dream of such an outcome. You can almost hear Tracy saying, "Mom and Dad, this one's for you."

NOW IT'S YOUR TURN. . . .

So, after living vicariously through the epics of these thirty-one daunt-less, cunning-as-heck women, after experiencing their morning-till-night go-getting triumphs, their devastating face plants, and their climbs back out of the ditch, how could you not be fired up to GO RUN THE WORLD?!

Consider this your trusty toolbox for whatever venture you start. With these tips, plus your high-wattage brain, you have everything you need to dive in IMMEDIATAMENTE (that's Italian for NOW!). Read on for a primer that covers essential basics.

YOUR ULTIMATE BUSINESS SURVIVAL KIT
Sixteen Must-Know Concepts

1. BUSINESS PLAN. A business plan is a lot like the written outline your teacher insists you do before beginning a history report. It's a brief summary of your idea and how you will execute it. The plan also covers the market size (see page 266), what makes your concept different and better, your target customer, the competition, sales projections (i.e., how many units of your product you imagine you'll sell in the first year and beyond), and a financial plan for how you'll handle money coming in and money going out, as well as biographies of the founder(s). The *real* value of this document isn't the summary on paper but the act of sitting down and planning everything out. A business plan is usually fifteen to twenty pages; it's what's handed to venture capitalists to snag your first meeting and hopefully some cash. Sometimes, instead of a printed report, founders will create a digital **pitch deck,** essentially a slideshow format to deliver the same info.

Before writing a full business plan, it's smart to do a preliminary one-pager to get the basics down. Then you build from there. (See page 278 for a sample single-page business plan.)

2. MARKET SIZE. This is the number of people who could potentially buy your product. You see, the group of people who might spend their money on your karaoke app or fringe earrings is a subset of the whole planet. So to estimate your universe of possible purchasers, you use available data—plus some assumptions, educated guesses, and math— to arrive at a figure.

Market size matters because it indicates how large an opportunity exists for your business. When Sara at Spanx needed to convince factories to produce her underwear, her top selling point was the massive market size, which meant big orders for the manufacturer! Sara believed that every woman age twenty to seventy was a potential Spanx buyer. They generally all wear underwear (well, maybe a few go commando, but mostly!), and they generally all care about how they look in clothes. She reasoned that before age twenty, women wouldn't be thinking about body jiggle and wouldn't feel a need for Spanx, and the over-seventy ladies were too set in their ways to try her novel underthings. So what was her market size? Using US population data, she calculated roughly 105 million women were her potential customers.

From there, she could figure out how many Spanx she was likely to sell. Even though 105 million women were possible buyers, not all of them would actually buy. See, some women couldn't afford Spanx, others wouldn't like the feel of the fabric, and some would just never hear about the product. She optimistically estimated that she could turn 75 percent of women in her market into buyers—she *really* believed in the awesomeness of her invention! That 75 percent figure is termed market penetration, and in Sara's case, it worked out to 79 million women.

Her next step was to figure how many actual pairs of Spanx she could sell. She did this by slicing up her likely-customer "pie" into pieces based on various types of shoppers. Half, she believed, would be experimenters—they would buy one pair just to see what Spanx was all about. One-quarter would see Spanx as the answer to their prayers and buy five right away, one for every day of the workweek! And one-quarter would get two, because they were enthused and worried the product would sell out. Calculating all that, she believed she could sell about 180 million pairs of Spanx.

3. COMPETITIVE ADVANTAGE. Competitive advantage is the aspect of your business that allows you to beat out your rivals. It is the fundamental reason a customer would choose to get their dark chocolate fix from Diane at the Candy Store, say, instead of at a drugstore, even though the sweets are pricier at the Candy Store and require trekking across town. The Candy Store stocks dozens of varieties of dark chocolate, from malt balls to French nougat olives. The shop is visually gorgeous, and Diane, the owner, asks about your day and gives free tastes, so the whole *experience* is sweet. The Candy Store's competitive advantage is that elevated feeling you get when you go, that you're important, that the chocolate is made just for you. For Kara at Hint, her water-and-sunscreen company's competitive advantage is that the products have no bad chemicals and others do.

4. A MISSION BEYOND MONEY. Nothing boosts sales more than a customer's emotional bond to your company. This happens most powerfully when your business stands for something beyond moneymaking. When a customer buys one of Jane's baby blankets at Little Lotus, they get a cozy infant wrap that promotes sleep, *and* they help give a premature baby access to one of the low-cost incubators produced by Jane's nonprofit Embrace Innovations, following the One for One model popularized by TOMS shoes (see page 93): for every purchase, one is donated to a person or place in need. In the case of Little Lotus, some of the proceeds from each blanket go toward buying an incubator to be donated to a hospital or clinic in the developing world. This makes Little Lotus stand out—and makes customers feel particularly good about their purchase.

Sword & Plough is also working toward loftier ideals than just profits. Emily's company exists not only to sell bags but also to push for recycling and environmental health and to promote respect for veterans. For you, the entrepreneur, solving a societal problem with your business can motivate you and your customer. What is your mission beyond money?

5. PATENT. A patent is a way of protecting an invention for a period of time (twenty years in the United States) so no one can copy you. Remember how Sara at Spanx chopped the legs off her pantyhose and then wrote her own patent? To be granted a patent, you must jump through some serious hoops: You must be the first person to file a patent for this idea. You must explain how *everything* about the product works and is made. And you need to prove that there is no "prior art," meaning you must show that the idea is not already in use or for sale. Also, for a patent, your invention has to be practically doable (time travel cannot be patented, for instance). It must also be nonobvious to an expert (for example, a toothbrush invented for cleaning teeth is totally obvious and will not get a patent today). The patent office only wants to issue patents on *new* ideas.

To file a patent, first research whether anyone has already patented your idea. Research the web, newspapers, and the patent database on the US Patent and Trademark Office website (uspto.gov). Sometimes businesses choose not to patent because doing so requires publishing all the secrets for making that product. Other people can then learn how Sara made her original Spanx undergarment (fabric, waistband, dimensions, etc.) and use this information to create something better to compete with her. People weigh the value of twenty years of protection against the benefit of keeping their secrets hush-hush. Here is Sara's original Spanx patent, so you can see what one looks like for real.

United States Patent [19]

Blakely

[10]   **Patent No.:   US 6,276,176 B1**

[45]   **Date of Patent: Aug. 21, 2001**

[54]   **PANTYHOSE UNDER GARMENT**

[76]   Inventor: Sara T. Blakely, 800-A E. Morningside Dr., Atlanta, GA (US) 30324

(*) Notice: Subject to any disclaimer, the term of this patent is extended or adjusted under 35 U.S.C. 154(b) by 0 days.

[21]   Appl. No.: 09/544,829

[22]   Filed: Apr. 6, 2000

[51]   Int. Cl. (^7) D04B 9/46; A41B 11/14

[52]   U.S. Cl. . . . . 66/178 R

[58]   Field of Search . . . . 66/116 R, 171, 66/178 R, 182, 183, 185, 178 A; 450/101, 104, 156; 2/239, 240

[56]   **References Cited**

     U.S. PATENT DOCUMENTS

     4,351, 068 9/1982 Taylor
     4,862, 523 * 9/1989 Lipov 2/409
     5,097,537 * 3/1992 Ewing 2/409
     5,465,894 * 11/1995 Imboden et al. 66/177
     6,151,927 * 11/2000 Owens et al. . . . . 66/178 R
     * cited by examiner

Primary Examiner—Danny Worrell

[74]   Attorney, Agent, or Firm—Morris, manning & Martin, L.L.P.

[57]   **ABSTRACT**

A pantyhose garment is provided that has relatively sheer leg portions that end with knitted-in wells just below or above the kneesm and a reinforced control top portion having good shaping and control characteristics that terminates at the top o the waist region with a kintted-in welt. The pantyhose under garment provides the user with shaping support, and because the lower leg is bare, it gives the user freedom to wear any type of shoe (i.e., open-toed-shoes, sandals, etc.). Pantyhose worn with open-toed shoes are usually undesirable, and also dangerous because the foot may slip in the shoe due to lack of friction between the panthose and the shoe. In addition, there are many occasions when the user wants a more casual look in clothing, and therefore pantyhose on the foot and ankle would not be desired. The reinforced control top portion extendds down the leg portions of the pantyhose far enough to provide support over the "saddlebag" and cellulite regions into the control top without causing waist constriction. Similary, the knitted-in welts at the ends of the leg portions blend into the leg portions without causing leg constriction. The overall design provides the user with a smooth, tight appearance when worn under clothing, without causing the user to suffer discomfort.

      20 Claims, 2 Drawing Sheets

6. TRADEMARK. A trademark is kind of like a patent, but the protection covers a word, a phrase, or even a package design. Tina has filed to trademark *Brandless* for use on her many snacks, cosmetics, and household products. Trademarking is handled by the US Patent and Trademark Office (USPTO), where one applies to secure something for exclusive use. There are two different symbols that are used in trademarking: TM and ®. The TM indicates that a company is seeking to claim that word, for example, for exclusive use in a particular category, such as apparel or candy, but has not yet been given the official thumbs-up from the USPTO. The ®, meaning registered trademark, which you see with Coca-Cola® and Snickers®, for instance, indicates that the trademark has been officially granted, so absolutely no copycatting!

The reason to use the TM before a trademark is legally issued is to dissuade others from using that language or design. Wildfang uses TM to "own" their phrase *Wild Feminist* for use on jackets and shirts. In Wildfang's case, even with TM, the phrase was still copied by a big retailer and put on T-shirts. Emma was so peeved that she posted on Instagram, "please stop ripping us off #trademarkinfringement." The store did respond, and took the shirt off their website. To file a trademark, search the USPTO database to see if one already exists. If it doesn't, fill out an application using the Trademark Electronic Application System. The fee is $225 to $400, depending on the type.

7. ECONOMIES OF SCALE. Economies of scale work like this: The more you buy of an item, the cheaper it gets. If you want to get your sweat on at SoulCycle and you buy a single-class pass, you pay $32. If you are intent on getting in better shape and spring for the 20-class pass at $580, your per-class price drops to $29. Commit to 30 cycles, and your cost is just $28 per class. SoulCycle gives a bulk discount to incentivize people to commit to becoming spin studio regulars. They know that once you come a few times in a row, which you are likely to do if you have prepaid, you get hooked. (Remember how it's a bit cult-ish?) Selling this way also makes SoulCycle better able to predict their rider numbers, which helps with scheduling, company growth, and financial planning. So for customers and entrepreneurs, buy in bulk where possible. If you start a school supply biz, a big box of pencils is going to be much cheaper per pencil than a three-pack. Just buy the jumbo size, split them up, and pocket the savings.

8. NETWORKING. If ski racers thrive on technical skills like edging and balance, stellar entrepreneurs win with people skills. Networking is simply meeting and talking to tons of people, to make connections, strike deals, find employees, and more. You can't be shy. Well, you can, but please don't let it stop you from networking. Get gutsy, and you'll see a major payoff. Try this: Seek out anyone who has more experience than you in your subject. Say you are launching a chocolate wedding cake business. Find people who run bakeries, or bake stacks of cakes, or work in another part of the wedding business. What are all the things you can ask? If you are looking to drum up customers for your new flower business, start with your parents' friends, your neighbors, and maybe your neighbor's new interior decorator.

9. CROWDFUNDING. This is a legit way to ask complete strangers to send you money. What?! Count me in! The underlying concept is that lots and lots of little donations add up to mucho money quickly. The internet makes it possible to use the power of crowds to do more collectively than any one person, or a few people, could ever do on their own. The first big crowdfunding sites (Kickstarter, GoFundMe, Indiegogo, etc.) started around 2012; now, every day, young entrepreneurs post their ideas to these sites, describing their products and their unique mission and the amounts they need in order to succeed, and the sites help spread the word. If all goes well, money just drifts out of clear blue sky into open hands. You must be eighteen years old to post your project, but you can get around this by having your parent or teacher sponsor your campaign. To stand out, make a compelling written or video pitch. Explain—with verve!—why your product is better than all the rest (competitive advantage!). You can post your business plan if you want. Then publicize your campaign among friends and family using Facebook and Instagram. You can even offer a prize, like doughnuts or a school cafeteria serenade, to everyone who forwards your link to twenty people.

10. ANGEL INVESTORS. Angel investors fund very young companies. They tend to invest small amounts (between $5,000 and $50,000), often referred to as **seed funding.** The "seeds" are the funds they sprinkle to many companies, hoping some will take root and grow into ginormous, profitable "trees." The term *angel* is used because these early funders often make or break a company's ability to even get going—to live or die, so to speak.

11. VENTURE CAPITAL. Venture capital (VC) is a type of funding used to help high-potential companies grow quickly. In exchange for giving you money when your business is risky, a venture capital firm becomes a part owner of your company. That works for the VC because if your company booms, it becomes more valuable, and they now own a slice of that larger pie. Venture capital funding is quite difficult to raise, and just 15 percent of VC dollars in 2017 went to start-ups with at least one female founder on the team. But take heart! Many people are trying to understand why and to improve those odds. An initiative called All Raise (allraise.org) is a group of women VCs who have pledged to increase the portion of VC dollars going to female-led start-ups to 25 percent in ten years, while also doubling the percentage of women who are VCs themselves.

The VC fund-raising process starts with networking to get introduced to one of these individuals or firms. Know someone who raised VC funding? Maybe they could connect you. Next, send them your business plan, explaining why your idea is huge and amazing with massive growth potential, why the time is *now,* and why you are just the gal to be CEO. If they are intrigued, you may be invited to share your idea in more detail.

12. ELEVATOR PITCH. No entrepreneur gets going without a perfect elevator pitch. The elevator pitch is your quick sales spiel, meaning it should take no longer than an elevator ride to say out loud (twenty to thirty seconds). You need to treat this pitch like your do-or-die moment. Deliver your pitch with gusto and urgency. You will use it again and again, so make it hum (and tap-dance).

Here's one version Katrina used for Stitch Fix: *Stitch Fix is a personal stylist that's brought to your door. We use online tools so you can let us know what your size and style preferences are. We'll have a stylist choose five things for you to try on at home. You simply buy what you want and send back what you don't. Just pay for what you keep.*

It's meant to make personal shopping, which used to be very much a luxury, accessible to everyday women, and men and kids as well.

13. TAKING A LOAN. The majority of ventures need money to get going. Many entrepreneurs start by asking parents or other family members for a loan. Loans have an important catch—lenders (other than some parents, maybe) charge for the trouble of giving you those funds. Because you have their money, they can't spend it elsewhere, which is a potential cost for them. So they charge a little extra for that, and for their risk. (Suppose you don't pay them back?) This extra cost is called **interest.** Banks always charge interest on a loan. The interest rate for small-business loans is around 4 to 6 percent. So let's say you take a $1,000 bank loan. The amount you need to pay back at the end of a set period is the $1,000 at 4 percent interest, called the **principal,** plus the interest, which is 4 percent of 1,000 (.04 x 1,000), or $40. For your $1,000 loan, you would need to hand over $1,040. Don't forget about that extra $40 when figuring your **costs**!

14. PR. This stands for public relations, which means the work of managing the relationship between a business and the public. This is necessary because it helps shape how people think of a particular company or product, which will impact whether they will buy that dress or visit that cycle studio.

Often the main objective of PR is to gain attention. From people in the subway. From news crews so you land on TV. From that girl everyone at school idolizes and copies. Customers have oodles of choices, so standing out is essential for attracting buyers or users. Or sometimes a concept is very new, so PR helps consumers to understand what your business is. This was the case for 23andMe, which was offering the first-ever personal genetic test. Since Anne wanted at-home DNA testing to be understood, and 23andMe to be recognized, she threw spit parties. What a bizarre idea! Because the concept was so weird, the media jumped to share it. When they spotlighted celebrities spitting, they also explained the basics of personal genetic tests, which helped Anne introduce her concept to the public.

15. DELIGHT THE CUSTOMER. Sometimes the smallest things make the biggest difference to customers. Life can be routine, and everybody loves unexpected gestures and fun surprises. When companies pop these into your day, often costing them very little, the payoff is huge. Natasha at Coolhaus sells an awful lot of her ice cream sandwiches out of her trucks, which means there are often no trash cans, so what to do with the plastic wrapper is a universal pain. In a moment of brilliance, she thought, Wouldn't it be great to make the packaging edible, and then you could just pop it into your mouth, no muss no fuss? With a little research, she found a manufacturer to create wraps using potatoes flattened into paperlike sheets. Because customers had never eaten their *whole* treat before and this was so eco-smart, she got people buzzing about how cool Coolhaus was, creating lots of loyalty and love for her brand. What will you do to surprise and thrill your customers?

16. WEBSITE DOMAIN. To have a website, you need to own the domain, which is a specific website address. You do this by purchasing an address from one of the many domain sellers online, such as GoDaddy, Domain, Bluehost, iPage, HostGator, and so on—there are many, and any will do. All domain sellers are connected to a single centralized registry, operated by ICANN (Internet Corporation for Assigned Names and Numbers).

On the domain site, enter the name you would like for your website in the search bar. The site will then tell you whether that name is available. It is best to get a dot-com address, rather than .us, .co, or .net, because these variations are not yet standard, and people could have a hard time finding your website. So if the-name-you-choose.com has been claimed, then it's probably best to pick another name. With Go-Daddy, domain registration costs $11.99 for one year, and then there's an annual renewal fee. If someone owns the name you want, you can try to buy it from them. By searching at whois.net, you can learn who owns that address, get their contact information, and reach out to ask. Minted CEO Mariam did this for her first company, Eve.com, first contacting a little girl named Eve who owned that address, and ultimately convincing her to sell by offering her free trips and fun perks. (One was making little Eve an honorary Eve.com board member, though she never attended any meetings!)

PUTTING IT DOWN ON PAPER

Writing a Very Preliminary Business Plan

Doing a basic one-page business plan is a great way to solidify your idea. It's also useful for communicating your concept to others—maybe a friend you are wooing to partner with you, or a parent you're hitting up for a small loan. A single sheet, even peanut-butter-smudged and scribbled in pencil, provides a scaffolding to build on. From there, you fill in more and more info, until you have a fully detailed blueprint, ready to send to a potential funder or share with a target client or retail store. This short-format starter plan will force you to boil your business down to its essence, which should help you clarify your ideas.

Does your idea feel like a too-hot French fry in your mouth, desperate to be spit OUT into the world? Good. Then you're ready to start! Take a stab at filling in the sample business plan on the next page.

BUSINESS PLAN FOR _____

(YOUR COMPANY NAME GOES HERE)

OVERVIEW

Describe your business idea in one sentence: _____

_____

COMPETITIVE ADVANTAGE

What is unique about your offering?_____

_____

CUSTOMERS/MARKET SIZE

Who will buy your product?_____

How many of these customers are there?_____

How many/how much will each customer buy?_____

MARKETING

How will you get customers to notice you?_____

_____

OBSTACLES

Who are your main competitors?_____

What are the barriers to getting into this business?_____

_____

What are the risks?_____

MONEY

How much will you charge for your product?_____

What is your target for sales in year one? In year two?_____

Estimate your costs._____

Estimate your profits (sales minus costs)._____

How much money do you need to get started?_____

PEOPLE

Why are you the best person to do this? _____

_____

What special skills do you bring?_____

_____

DIVING INTO THE FINANCES

Now the big fun begins—tracking the money, moolah, coin, green-backs, etc. Riches! Profits! Bills to pay! Oh my!

This is where things get real.

There are some basic financial concepts every enterprising business gal must know to stay afloat. First, you need to know how to keep track of your sales; your costs, or expenses (like employee salaries and the materials to make your product); and your profits (what you really make after subtracting your expenses). If you start a product-based company, you will need to manage inventory (the goods you are planning to sell—candy, beanies, fizzy bath bombs, whatever). You need money to acquire that inventory (to pay for the raw material, the transportation, the warehousing, etc.), and you need this money before you sell anything, which makes it tricky (how do you make money before you have something to sell?). But without cash flow—money coming in and going out in some kind of balance—you won't make it.

Keeping track of money can get messy. Fortunately, there are special charts and conventions to help you. Let's start with an example.

A Peek Inside the Yellowberry
Bra Business

A good way to learn financial fundamentals is to study a real business. Let's take Yellowberry, the bra company seventeen-year-old Megan Grassell started in Jackson Hole, Wyoming, in 2013.

Megan's inspired idea was born when she took her little sis Mary Margaret shopping for her first bra. The offerings horrified them both— there was almost nothing available but leopard push-up styles and sexy lacy numbers, all with underwire galore. The styles felt so inappropriate for a self-conscious girl just getting her figure. Megan knew she could do better. She chose to call her start-up Yellowberry because many near-ripe berries are yellow, and girls getting their first bras are in that same in-between, near-mature state. She thought up all kinds of fun marketing ideas for her brand, which would stand for real girls being their authentic selves. Staying true to the "real" concept, she decided to use actual customers and friends of Mary Margaret as models. Snapshots of the girls in bras would be taken from the back only, to minimize any overexposed feeling. Megan's idea was way bigger than her product. "This is such a bigger mission than a cotton bra. Can I build a brand that's supporting girls growing up—not rushing them?" she mused. Megan's sales began slowly but eventually got cranking. She succeeded in getting into Nordstrom, until she pulled out, deciding they demanded too high a percentage of the price per bra. Now she's entered a new partnership with the largest department store in Asia, and she sells online.

But before *any* of this, Megan sketched a simple design on a yellow legal pad, bought some stretchy fabric, and brought it to a seamstress. "She goes 'Where's your pattern?'" Megan recalled. "So we made one right then out of construction paper." Then, with a sample in hand, Megan made one cold call after another to factories until one in Los Angeles agreed to produce bras in small quantities (now Yellowberry is the manufacturer's largest customer!).

Okay, that's the backstory. Now let's take a deep dive into the money part of launching Yellowberry. Some of the numbers here have been simplified or changed to keep the example straightforward and easy to follow.

The factory looked at Megan's sample, or prototype, and quoted a $10 manufacturing cost for each bra. The cost included the fabric plus the labor (factory workers' time). Megan calculated that packaging and shipping added 50¢ per bra. So the cost to make and ship each bra was $10.50. This is called cost of product. To start her business, Megan had $4,200 in savings from her longtime hostess job and her work in a gas station.

Megan figured that if she used all her savings, she could afford to have the factory sew 400 bras ($4,200 divided by $10.50 = 400). Once she made money from those 400, she could produce more, and sell more, and so on, until she was BRA QUEEN of North America. She would offer three sizes (S, M, L), and she wanted blue and yellow (B, Y) color choices in each size. That meant six different kinds of bra (SB, SY, MB, MY, LB, LY). She calculated that she should order 66 of each kind (400 divided by 6 kinds = 66 of each).

To estimate her profits, she needed to figure out her pricing and all of her business costs.

So, pricing: How much should she charge for her bras? Pricing is as much an art as a science. There were several things to consider. First, what did competitive bras cost? Second, what were all the costs involved in making and selling the bras? She needed to make sure those costs were covered before she could make money. Megan did some online research, looking at other starter bras girls might buy, from Victoria's Secret, Gap, Target, and so on. Considering the offerings, Megan set the price for her Budding Berry Bra at $29.95. She aimed to be midrange price-wise. She didn't need to be the cheap choice because she was offering something novel: a simple, well-fitting, age-appropriate bra. And that midrange price would cover her $10.50 cost per bra and leave her a reasonable **margin.** The margin is the difference between the price charged for a product and the cost of making the product.

For a $29.95 bra that cost $10.50 to produce and ship, Megan's margin is $19.45. Margin is an important metric used to evaluate a business. It is not, however, Megan's profit. That's because the cost of the product is not the only cost involved in running Yellowberry. Other costs must also be subtracted to determine profit.

The other costs of operating Megan's business are called **operating expenses.**

Here they are for 2014:

Office rent	**$0** (she was working from home)
Website domain	**$12**/year
Salary	**$0** (year one, she wasn't paying herself)
Cell phone bill	**$350**/year
Plane ticket and Uber to visit the factory	**$375**
Office supplies	**$25**
Marketing materials	**$250**
Total Operating Expenses	**$1,012**

We will put her sales, cost of product, and operating expenses together in one document used to calculate profits, called an **income statement.** That financial document starts with recording sales, so let's look at Megan's sales.

Megan uploaded photos to her website before announcing on Facebook "Yellowberry has launched! Come, bring your boobs. Cute bras for sale!" The first week she sold one lonely bra (to her dad—UGH!). The next month, she sold three. Then she launched a Kickstarter campaign (see pages 271–272) with a goal of $25,000. Donations came in slowly at first, but after a week, at the end of a full day without internet access while traveling to Guatemala for a school trip, she logged on to find donations going nuts. She burst into tears. A site called A Mighty Girl had recommended Yellowberry, and that did it. All her donors bought a bra, so all 400 bras in her inventory sold. She raised $29,365 in company funding on top of the money from her sales. Cool beans!

She calculated her sales by multiplying the price per bra times the number of bras sold ($29.95 × 400 bras = $11,980). On the income statement we'll put sales and costs—both operating and cost of production—together to show her profit in year one.

INCOME STATEMENT FOR YELLOWBERRY

For the year ending 31 December 2014

REVENUE	
Bra sales	$11,980
Cost of Product	$4,200
Margin	**$7,780**
OPERATING EXPENSES	
Office rent	$0
Website domain	$12
Salary	$0
Cell phone bill	$350
Plane ticket and Uber to factory	$375
Office supplies	$25
Marketing materials	$250
Total Operating Expenses	**$1,012**
PROFIT	**$6,768**

After paying all her expenses, Megan had made $6,768 in profit! Hurray! With her Kickstarter blowout, Megan knew customers wanted her bras. Next, she had to decide how many bras to produce in the next order. She knew she had to keep enough money aside for a growing set of upcoming expenses—as sales grow, so do expenses. For instance, she needed to update her website functionality to make it easier for customers to purchase her product. She needed to hire an afternoon helper. "Okay, I have thousands of orders, standardized tests for college applications, calculus homework—help me pack boxes!" she recalls feeling at the time.

And now we're back to where we started this case study: thinking about cash, and the timing of it into and out of Yellowberry's bank account—or **cash flow.** Having money on hand to pay bills is where cash flow comes in. Once Yellowberry started really cranking, it would be impossible to wait for all the money from bra sales to hit the bank account before paying monthly bills and ordering even more bras. If Megan always waited for all the sales cash to order more bras, there would be a lag for customers, because sewing the bras takes several months. Then, when customers went online, no bras would be available. Not having product is simply called A DISASTER because customers go elsewhere and may never come back.

Fortunately, the Kickstarter campaign was very successful, so Megan had that big wad of cash as a cushion. Now she had her $6,768 profits, plus $29,365 in donations. To monitor all this cash, she used a **cash flow statement.**

CASH FLOW STATEMENT FOR YELLOWBERRY

For the year ending 31 December 2014

CASH FLOW FROM OPERATIONS

(amounts in parentheses mean money going out)

Cash from bra customers	$11,980
Cash paid to supply bras	($4,200)
Cash paid for operating expenses	($1,012)
Net cash flow from operations	**$6,768**

CASH FLOW FROM FINANCING ACTIVITIES

Cash from Kickstarter	$29,365
Net cash flow from financing activities	**$29,365**
NET INCREASE IN CASH	**$36,133**

With $36,133 in cash in the Yellowberry bank account, Megan decided to triple her next order to 1,200 bras. Up front, then, she needed to pay the factory $10 x 1,200, or $12,000, for the bras. She needed to pay 50¢ x 1,200 for packaging and shipping, so $600. Her website upgrade was a big investment. It would cost $10,000. That took her cash down to $13,533 ($36,133–$12,000–$600–$10,000). There were also operating expenses, like another trip to the factory to check on production, phone bills, etc. As she went, she would produce new quarterly cash flow statements to be sure she had the cash she needed to pay her bills.

With a very basic understanding of the income statement, the cash flow statement, and the process for calculating margin and profits, you have some of the tools you will need for planning and for tracking how your business is doing. Keep your calculator close and your columns straight and you will be IN BUSINESS!

YOUNG ENTREPRENEUR-TESTED/APPROVED IDEAS

So, you're inspired, but you're wondering: Can a novice like me really do this? Yes. YES! But it's not a bad idea to start small, with something you can pull off fairly easily. Treat your first business like an experiment. Learn everything you can from it. Once you've proven your dominance in the field, sell (or hand off) the business to a worthy person; then take on a riskier, bolder business for your second endeavor.

But what should your first business be? Will lightning strike and hand you the perfect idea? Probably not. It's more likely that you'll need to take some of these steps to find your idea:

Start an "idea club." Debbie Sterling, who was a total business newbie when she founded her toy company, GoldieBlox, held a weekly "Idea Brunch" with her pals. They'd sit around and share business concepts they were kicking around and give each other feedback. You can do this, too. If the group is having trouble conjuring up ideas, consider motivational treats (Swedish Fish have been known to stoke the imagination!).

Make a hassle list. A surefire way to put yourself into business is to do smilingly for others the tasks that they most dread. To figure out those most-hated life to-dos, make a hassle list. Here, let's get you started: Cleaning the fish skin off the barbecue. Weeding. Picking up dog poop. Returning bad online purchases. Unjamming the printer. Cleaning crud/toe jam out from under toenails. No, not every annoyance can lead to a business opportunity for you, entrepreneur girl (Dirty toenails? Leave that one to the salon, please!), but many can! Call of Doodie Pet Waste Removal had one thirteen-year-old plugging his nose and then rolling in dough. The only tools he needed were rubber gloves, plastic bags, and some dog treats for safely invading backyards! Printer meltdown got your neighbor bumming? Rent yourself out as an hourly in-home techie for everyday impossibilities like recording TV shows, programming the remote, connecting printers to computers—if a person is over fifty, chances are they struggle with all or some of these issues. Dirty jobs that need to happen weekly are ideal. Compost bin scrubber, anyone?

Put a twist on a proven idea. Lemonade stands almost always make money—a little, at least. What else could you sell at a table to people just walking by? Get zany with your ideas! Jam jars full of chicken noodle soup to take home for dinner? Bins of fresh strawberries that you got by the pallet at a nearby farm? Bottled water, sunscreen, and visors by the beach? Coffee and doughnuts at sporting events? Sometimes it's just a twist on a proven idea that makes all the difference.

Shrink it! One of the twists to consider is a youth-oriented version of something already popular with adults. The Skimm is an extremely popular roundup of daily news (founded by a pair of female entrepreneurs) told in a light, easy-to-digest newsletter format. What about launching the young-person version—call it the Skittle—a fun, colorful digest of local gossip written by and for middle graders? Or what about a Yelp-style website with reviews of books, bands, sneaker styles, apps, and amusement parks? Another idea: Think of all the subscription box-of-the-month businesses like Dollar Shave Club and Birchbox. What could be shipped monthly to people your age?

Make a skills list. List all the things you are really, really good at. Does this list point to a certain kind of business? Are you an A student who should be tutoring? My daughter, Emma, can dance, ice-skate, sing, and do makeup (even cat eyes). She's an expert organizer and room cleaner. She's the queen of list making. She's adored by young kids. Her skill set is perfectly suited to entertaining kids at birthday parties, especially big parties where the parents are overloaded with tasks of their own. We've brainstormed this idea. She could become known around the neighborhood as the birthday helper who shows up with a bag of tricks (hair spray, tutus, a playlist on her phone, and a dance move to teach everyone). One day, if the business takes off, she could secure her own venue, and parties could come to her (for an extra charge, of course!).

Ellis Toole in Berkeley, California, followed her skill set and launched Ellis Handmade Jewelry while in junior high. She started with a trunk show at her mom's office, where she sold nine pairs of earrings. From there, she did bigger and bigger trunk shows, some a full weekend long and earning her around $9,000 (minus the cost of supplies). By the time she reached high school, a neighborhood boutique started stocking her jewelry. Then she launched an Etsy store. At times, prepping for a trunk show, she made jewelry until her fingers were covered in sores! Growing her business ("scaling," if you want the business term) was never a priority. "I prioritized the craftsmanship and uniqueness of each piece. I didn't want to just replicate bestsellers because I want the creative experience," she said. One problem was that she got so good at twisting wire and artfully beading, she couldn't ever find anyone as good as she was to hire to help her! She put her business (including her Etsy store) on a temporary break while she attends UC Berkeley for college but plans to open back up.

What are your special skills? Use them. What's bugging you? Fix it. Have you heard the story of eight-year-old Abbey of Makin Bacon? She was microwaving bacon in the family kitchen when they ran out of paper towels to sop up the grease. What we need, she said to her dad, is something that eliminates the need for towels—like a rack that sits inside a dish to collect the messy drippings. Her dad found a manufacturer who could make a prototype of her idea. Then he sent a picture of Abbey and her invention to *O* and lots of other magazines, which resulted in many articles and even convinced a bacon manufacturer to feature the rack on its package. Abbey and her dad sold millions of them.

Peaches and Kate have a similar story. A pair of San Francisco teens who'd been friends forever found themselves on a beach in Hawaii in 2017, wondering why all the bathing suits around them were so lame. They made some drawings and paid a seamstress to make a sample. It didn't look so good, and it cost them a whopping $70, so the girls reluctantly learned to sew. Within months, they had sold about 100 made-to-order swim tops and bottoms—almost all of them to their eighth-grade friends and friends' friends. Customers got to pick their color, size, and style. Peaches and Kate has already earned its founders enough to buy two $500 sewing machines and one $800 embroidery machine for sewing on logos. They sell their suits online and have been picked up by a Hawaiian retailer. And they both just started ninth grade! Problem solved.

And here's one more problem solver who's running for the bank: Middle school lacrosse defender Rachel Zietz, age thirteen, was tossing dirty lacrosse balls against the walls of her Florida house and driving her parents nuts when her idea popped into her mind. The walls were getting dirty because the rebounder out in her yard (a taut net that bounces balls back so you can practice throwing and catching) was rusty and loose. She thought, How hard could it be to make a reasonably priced rebounder that is weatherproof and stays bouncy? She borrowed $30,000 from her parents (she has paid them back!), found a manufacturer, and enrolled in a young entrepreneur's program through the Boca Raton Chamber of Commerce. Rachel sold $200,000 in rebounders in her first year and expanded into making goals, sticks, and other lacrosse accessories. At fifteen, she made a thrilling appearance pitching for funding on the ABC show *Shark Tank.* Though she didn't get funding at that time, she persevered. Now Gladiator Lacrosse has solid sales and is supplying the official goals for the 2018 Men's World Lacrosse Championship.

What is annoying you that *you* can improve? What do you need? What do you care about? Could be something small, like scrunchies. Or something political, like gun control in schools or preserving our planet. What current trends do you gravitate toward? Did you know that a lot of investors look at kids your age as trend weathervanes? When investors saw kids getting so into video games, they jumped on the whole e-sports phenomenon. Long before launching RewardStyle, Amber, the founder, noticed style blogs popping up everywhere. She had one, and so did lots of her friends. Ding! A business was born. Jesse at Lumi launched her sun-activated T-shirt dyes right into the heart of the Maker Movement because she recognized, early, that DIY is here to stay and that she had something to offer the marketplace. Notice the trends around you and your business ideas will follow.

Still stumped about where to start and what to start? Here are a few business concepts developed by people under age sixteen that have worked recently around the United States and that you can adapt to make bank in your own town:

The School Supply Hack: Every August, the school supply list arrives, popping the blissful bubble of responsibility-free summer. Driving to three superstores to find 3"x5" cards blank on one side and lined on the other, plus the pencil bag that clips into the three-ring binder, is a HASSLE. (How many heavy sighs does your mom or dad heave doing this?) Ding. You've identified a problem you can solve. Become the school supply fairy!

Handle the supply shopping and deliver required items, neatly packaged, to each classmate's doorstep! This idea came from a kid in Mill Valley, California, and it's a hot one. Start by searching online for the best prices. Remember, things get cheaper when purchased in bulk, so that's another way beyond convenience that parents win by using your service. In your promotional flyer or email, cite how much they will save on the protractor (or ruler or spare pencil lead) by buying through you. By pricing things out and comparison shopping before ordering, you'll figure out what you need to charge to cover the goods and earn a little extra for your work.

Locate a school directory for addresses, and contact everyone in the grade and their parents. If they want to participate, get a firm commitment before ordering supplies so you know how much to buy. Play up the pain you are sparing them (even calculate that you will save them three 45-minute trips, for instance, for a grand total schlep savings of 135 minutes plus gas!). Once the big boxes of binders and #2 pencils start arriving, set up a war room where you can fill orders. Consider paying a friend or your little sis to help stuff packets. Tie each with a ribbon so the packages look professional. Payment could be to you by check or by PayPal or Venmo. If you don't have any savings to use, you might need to collect payment in advance in order to have cash to buy the supplies.

Heartstrings-Pulling Highlight Reel: Spend any time on the sidelines of youth sports fields and you will feel the rabid involvement parents have with their mini (but Olympic-bound, surely) athletes. Parents never miss a game. They hoot and swear like there's money to be won. The future Alex Morgan is *their* kid. No surprise: Many parents shoot action sports pics.

Here's where you come in. There is a pile of money to be made packaging *every* season into a nostalgic slideshow and videos for team families. Throughout the season, mention to parents that you are collecting photos. Make little cards with your email to pass out, and lightly nudge parents at games to send you their snapshots. Later, if you aren't on the team, hit up someone who is, for a screenshot of the team roster to get members' emails. Organize the photos and videos you've collected in a folder on your computer desktop, particularly if they're for multiple teams. Using iPhoto or another program, make a slideshow with the images and video footage, and add music. Try recording some audio of team cheers on your phone and incorporate that, too. Now advertise the finished product to parents and players. You can send it out digitally as a file or save it to flash drives. If you do flash drives, add the cost of the drive into your price. One California teen charged $30 per family for such a video—so there's serious dough to be raked in!

Heartstrings-Pulling Party Reel (sidebar to the above): You can offer your highlight-reel services for any event that features photos, not just sports events. End-of-school-year party? Eighth-grade graduation? Sweet-sixteen bash? Bar or bat mitzvah? You could be rich by the first day of summer.

The Babysitters Club: Parents in your neighborhood surely need babysitting. Of course, you can post flyers and advertise on Nextdoor and Craigslist, offering yourself as facile with double Dutch, kickball, AND diapers. But here's a MUCH BIGGER idea for you: instead of becoming a plain-Jane single babysitter, organize a whole stable of babysitters, as in the Baby-sitters Club books. (Nina at EpiBone did this with her siblings, and now she's CEO of a breakthrough company that grows custom human bones.) Recruit friends who like kids. Insist that they take a babysitting class so they know first aid and CPR. Interview each pal to learn how often they want to work, their level of experience (can they sit for infants?), where they live, and when they're free. Make a spreadsheet with each babysitter and the days and hours they are available. Now advertise your sitter service. When parents call, you're sure to be able to staff their job because you have lots of sitters in your spreadsheet. Someone is likely free, and you will know who that is! As the organizer, you could charge the babysitters a few dollars for every job you get them. That's fair, since you are doing the work to get them hired! This model can also be used for a tutoring network or a dog-walking and pet-sitting enterprise.

Big-Game Garb: Every school, sports team, camp, and company has its BIG RIVAL. That's the one other group/team/company it can't stand to see win. Usually rival teams are crazy-competitive, which means any matchup draws crowds and generates max excitement. This is the perfect environment in which to sell team swag. How about printing a bunch of shirts with a clever slogan promoting one team or the other? The cleverer your slogans, the better! If you need ideas, host a slogan-brainstorming session with pizza and sundaes. Or go online and order a big box of noisemakers in team colors. Then show up at the big game with your wares and sell out!

Garage-Sale Guru: How about running garage sales for your neighbors? Leave flyers at nearby houses, offering to manage the whole affair from A to Z. Meet with the "client" in advance to see what they have in mind. Mark items for the sale with masking tape. Get the stuff organized. All the moving and prepping likely requires some heavy physical lifting, so consider partnering with someone (two can carry much more than one). Bring cleaning supplies. Make signs and price everything. Set up a table with a cash box and plenty of small bills for change. Make matching T-shirts for you and your partner(s) with your business name. Invest in a bubble machine or bake brownies to draw buyers. Have a stack of cards with your business name and contact information at checkout so people can book you for their next sale.

Moneymaking Machine: Pool your money with some friends and buy a snow-cone machine. Or a popcorn maker. Or a DJ setup. Or a movie projector for backyard showings on a sheet. Then open for business.

If you haven't gotten out a pen and circled something in this chapter, read it again and start circling. Somewhere in these final pages is the seed of an idea. Water it and see what grows.

NOW: GO RUN THE WORLD

You now have a whole parade of awesome role models. You've tapped the utimate brain trust, among the finest business minds on this big blue spinning globe of ours. Their wisdom and experience should be swirling around your noggin in an inspiring creative blizzard. A few keepsake gems should now be tucked in your front pocket for fast access. Like: Every business that is hella popular was once teeny and precarious, held together by paper clips and already-chewed gum. Remember, Coolhaus started with one engineless truck and one or two humdrum flavors made in a hand-crank machine in Natasha's nook of a kitchen. The Candy Store was once a measly little cart selling candy from jars at some friends' events. PopSugar and RewardStyle were blogs typed by one gal, usually while in her pj's.

Another must-remember gem: Perfectionism is waaaay overrated. It's for machines, not people, and certainly not for start-ups. Nothing is ever going to be neatly tied up in a bow, all lights green or flashing READY FOR LAUNCH. Ideas evolve, getting better mostly because things go wrong. Pals cute socks started as dueling crocheted animal mittens, which were a bust because the wares only sold in winter. But Hannah's opposing-character mittens spawned her mismatched socks. Sarah at

Nextdoor first toiled for TWO YEARS developing her sports fandom community, Fanbase, only to have to pull the plug. Mortifying! But all that angsting about online communities informed Nextdoor, now rocking in 190,000 neighborhoods.

There is no gold tincture or mystical potion that will suddenly conjure up a glorious company that produces lifelong bliss and $100 bills in towering stacks. The real trick to soaring as an entrepreneur is kinda boring: It's hard work, and more hard work. Also, refusing to take no for an answer, occasionally faking confidence, networking like crazy, getting back up when you're knocked down, and always just GOING FOR IT bravely and relentlessly.

Sara from Spanx added one more pearl on a recent podcast: Stop the negative self-talk. Simply tell yourself you *can* instead of listing reasons why you can't. It pays to sweep the naysayers and cynics from your life. They do to delicate, early ideas what sunlight does to vampires. Be kooky and contrarian, chasing the idea that everyone else deems nuts. Katrina at Stitch Fix talks about the fine line between brilliance and idiocy, and how great ideas all ride that line. "When you are doing something no one else is doing, you are either the smartest person in the room or the dumbest," she says. So stop judging yourself and ignore the people looking at you sideways and you'll be amazed at the breakthroughs that spring from your beauteous skull.

Before you go, here is a crucial final thought. Ask yourself the following question:

What would I do if I knew I could not fail?

Really, what would you do/start/chase like a starved rabbit if you believed you could not fail?

Let your answer be your true North Star, business girl. GO DO THAT. If you do, you will RUN THE WORLD.

GLOSSARY

BETA TEST: An early trial of your product or service, used to help improve the idea.

BOARD OF DIRECTORS: A group of people, appointed by a company's founder(s) and/or investors, who have expertise in various aspects of the business. They provide guidance in running the business and act as the CEO's boss.

CASH FLOW: The money coming into a business from sales and the money going out of the business to pay expenses. Tracking cash flow tells you how much money is on hand at any particular moment so you don't get caught unable to write your worker a check or hand a wad of cash to your factory to produce your socks.

CASH FLOW STATEMENT: The financial document that tracks all cash coming into and going out of a business during a particular time period.

COLD-CALL OR COLD-EMAIL: To communicate with a person or company you do not know at all, in hopes of getting a meeting, obtaining advice, developing a partnership, or selling them something.

COSTS: The money a company spends to operate, for things like salaries, inventory, office rent, and so on. Also commonly referred to as expenses.

CROWDFUNDING: A method of raising funds to start a business by asking for contributions, most typically via the internet, from friends, family, and strangers. Often donations are small, but a large number of these add up to a significant amount.

CROWDSOURCING: The practice of engaging a crowd, most typically via the internet, to work toward a common goal.

DEBT: Money that a business owes to a lender.

EXPENSES: Another word for costs, or the money a company spends to operate.

FDA: The Food and Drug Administration, which is the US government agency responsible for approving drugs, medical devices, and cosmetics, and for overseeing food safety.

HTML CODING: HTML is the standard computer language that tells a web page what to display on-screen. HTML stands for hypertext markup language.

INCOME STATEMENT: A financial document that records a company's sales and expenses over a specific time period.

INCUBATOR: A selective program run by successful entrepreneurs giving others much of what they need to transform a smart concept into a real business. Potential entrepreneurs are given expert guidance, office space, useful contacts, and occasionally a bit of funding.

INTEREST: The cost to the borrower for getting a loan. It is a percentage of the amount borrowed, due in addition to that amount.

INVENTORY: Product on hand, waiting to be sold by a business.

LAYOFF: Dismissal from a job for economic reasons.

LICENSE: An agreement to provide your technology or product for use by another business for a fee, almost like renting it to them.

MARGIN: The difference between the selling price of a product and the cost of producing that product.

NETWORKING: Actively seeking connections with people who can be helpful, with either advice, money, or introductions.

OPERATING EXPENSES: The everyday costs of running a business, from salaries and rent to electricity and toilet paper.

PITCH: A quick "sell" of your business idea, usually in the form of a super-fast, compelling presentation of the key concept, benefits, and financials.

PITCH COMPETITION: A contest in which entrepreneurs have typically a few minutes (sometimes even just one minute!) to sell their idea as persuasively as possible before judges in hopes of winning investment, an invitation into an incubator, prize money, or just bragging rights!

PITCH DECK: A written presentation of a business idea, often in the form of bullet-point slides, used to win investors or customers.

PIVOT: Shifting a company idea or strategy to make it better, often after receiving specific feedback or testing it with customers.

PRINCIPAL: The amount of money that is borrowed when a loan is taken out.

PROFIT: The money that a business makes after all expenses have been paid.

PROOF OF CONCEPT: Evidence from a small test (a pilot) that proves that a business idea is a good one.

PROTOTYPE: A rough model of an invention, usually from basic materials, created to understand how it will function and look.

REVENUE: The money that a business receives from selling its product during a specific time period, also referred to as sales.

SALES: The money that a business receives from selling its product during a specific time period, also referred to as revenue.

SEED FUNDING: A small investment given to a company early on to help them get off the ground, sometimes in exchange for a small ownership stake in the business. Often this money comes from friends, family, or an angel investor. The idea is to help the "seed" grow into a solid company.

SILICON VALLEY: A region south of San Francisco, around Stanford University, famous as the birthplace of technology giants like Apple and Google.

START-UP: A very young company that is just getting going.

STOCK EXCHANGE: A place where people buy and sell shares of public companies, also called stocks. In the United States, the major stock exchanges are the New York Stock Exchange and NASDAQ.

TAKE A COMPANY PUBLIC: The process of selling ownership in a business to the public as a way to raise money for expansion. Also called an initial public offering, or IPO. The company is divided into small parts of company stock, or "shares," which can then be traded between people on an exchange like the New York Stock Exchange or the NASDAQ.

TINKERING: The creative process of making an invention, usually involving experimentation and imaginative risk taking.

TRADE SECRET: A confidential special technique or tip a company uses because it provides them with an edge over competitors. Unlike a patent, a trade secret is not legally protected, but it is sometimes preferable to a patent because there is no requirement to publish the details.

WHOLESALE: The selling of a large number of goods at a discount to retailers, who will then sell them to customers.

ACKNOWLEDGMENTS

This book has been an exercise in following the wise advice of every entrepreneur in this book: *Boldly ask others for help.* Because the project sold in June and a draft was due in September, I was also constantly asking for those favors to happen *fast.* The generosity of time and spirit I have received has been overwhelming. In no particular order: Thank you, Danielle Svetcov, for being so excellent at what you do. Thank you, Kelsey Horton, for answering every last question and for seeing the vision so clearly. Beverly Horowitz, thank you for jumping at this idea. Caroline Paul, I owe you for giving me a model for a book for girls that really matters, and for constant encouragement. Wendy McNaughton, appreciation for creating Women Who Draw, your amazing platform showcasing female illustrators, which led me to Bijou. Bijou Karman, your illustrations are bold and fun and full of moxie, just like I wanted them to be. Thank you for working fast and being so talented. Thank you to my San Francisco Writers Grotto friends, my trusty writing community, for too many things to list. Many people helped me find my way to the women in the book. Thank you, Gaby Toledano, Amy Banse, Lindy Fishburne, Jan D'Alessandro, Jana Rich, Jack McDonald, Shelley Bransten, Tia Miller, Beth Scheer, Leticia Miranda, Staci Slaughter, Jenny Lefcourt, Ambar Bhattacharyya, Lisa Sugar, Natasha Lawler, and Jack McDonald. A special hat tip to Leslie Blodgett, whose positivity and can-do spirit I need to bottle and sell. For editing, ideas, inspiration, and sometimes just walking and listening, thank you, Lisa Kapp, Heidi Pennell, Rebecca Blumenstein, Jim Lesser, Tricia Lesser, Leela DeSouza Bransten, Diane Zoi, Jen Noland, Adina Safer, Kara Goldin, Jennifer Aaker, Anne Marie Burgoyne. Nina Howard, thank you for a valuable early read. For giving me clever kid businesses to feature, thank you, Leo Jacoby, Peaches Wright, Kate Garrity, Ellis Toole. A shout-out to Rodes Fishburne, who forces me to be confident even when I'm not feelin' it. Big appreciation to Nina Martin, who has always been my guide in this writing life. To Laura Youman Debole, your design talent is surely why my proposal sold. Izzy Pennell and Emma, thank you for summer research, editing, and being true power girls. Wanda Holland Greene, for being a gift to girls and my girl, and for your guidance and excitement. For your wordsmithing prowess, thank you, Elliot Singer. For help with blurbs, thank you, Katie Albright, Amy Low, Sheila Walker, Claire Shipman, Sophia Amoruso, Madeline Albright, Laurene Powell Jobs, Sam Altman, Arianna Huffington, and Gitanjali Rao. For bringing creative juice into our house always, and for your love, good humor, and steadiness, thank you Kapp Singer. For patience, big thinking, and the best ideas, always, David, I am simply the luckiest. And finally, big love to my EMC, the girls who literally run my world.